THE GREAT DISCOVERY

ULF AND BIRGITTA EKMAN

The Great Discovery

~

Our Journey to the Catholic Church

Translated by
Sister Clare Marie, O.C.D.

IGNATIUS PRESS   SAN FRANCISCO

Original Swedish title:
Den stora upptäckten—vår väg till katolska kyrkan
© 2015 by Ulf and Birgitta Ekman

English translation edited by David Michael

Frontispiece photograph by Rickard Eriksson

Cover photograph: The Dome of Saint Peter's Basilica
Photograph by Galen Crout

Cover design by Riz Boncan Marsella

ISBN 978-1-62164-222-0
Printed in 2018 by Ignatius Press, San Francisco
Library of Congress Control Number 2018931262
Printed in the United States of America ∞

We wish to dedicate this book especially to our four beloved sons. Through all the years, the love in our family has been our great joy and the point of reference in our lives. The family is God's wonderful gift to man, and we are eternally grateful for ours!

Contents

Foreword

by *Anders Cardinal Arborelius*

In the year 1989, Pope John Paul II visited Sweden. For many in our country, this visit was an eye-opener. People began shaking off centuries of anti-Catholic indoctrination and prejudice. This recently canonized pope awakened respect and inspired confidence. Not among everyone, however. I myself was present when the pope celebrated the Mass in Vadstena for the Catholic youth from all the Nordic countries. During a great part of the Mass, members of the Maranatha group could be heard in the distance crying out their hatred in choruses. Someone else who spoke out against the pope and his visit was Pastor Ulf Ekman from the Word of Life congregation in Uppsala. When the same Ulf Ekman was received into full communion with the Catholic Church twenty-five years later with his wife, Birgitta, it caused surprise and a lack of understanding in many. Much can happen in a quarter of a century. This book is a testimony to how two married people—and it is utterly essential to emphasize that these are two unique people, together, but nevertheless with full respect for the integrity of the other —went through a demanding and deep personal process of testing and conversion. These are two people filled with a deep longing for truth and nothing else. They had nothing to gain by becoming Catholics; quite the contrary. Their whole background as well as the situation of their lives, in which they had such an important position, contradicted that step which they have taken so decisively. From many sides, the reaction was strong and aggressive, and rightly so. When a free-church[1] leader, who is both highly esteemed by many and questioned by others, becomes Catholic, it stirs up strong reactions in our country, but when thousands of immigrant Catholics leave their faith for another, it never makes the headlines.

How did this journey begin? It is important to stress that it is a question of a very long and thorough process, a dedicated search for the whole truth that is revealed in Jesus Christ and that we, as Catholics, believe has been entrusted to the Catholic Church. The reader can imagine the power of God drawing people in different ways by the quiet murmuring of the Holy Spirit, who wants to open our hearts to all that he desires to give us. Step by step, Birgitta and Ulf describe this journey of discovery into the treasury of the Christian tradition. Saint Birgitta had an important role to play when the process began. "Show me the truth, and make me willing to walk in it." Birgitta's prophetic words are truly fulfilled in the path of her namesake today. It seems to be an undeniable sign of God's humor that both of these Birgittas were blessed with an Ulf for a spouse. Again, it must be pointed out that this book is not merely Ulf Ekman's, but that it is just as much Birgitta's. It is precisely because of this that it is also so unique. Classic conversion stories such as the *Confessions* of Saint Augustine, Saint Teresa of Avila's *Book of Her Life*, and John Henry Newman's *Apologia Pro Vita Sua* are the works of individual persons, as is also the book *The Holy Way of the Pilgrim*, by the seventeenth-century convert Lars Skytte. I was also struck by parallels between Ulf and

---

[1] A non-Lutheran Protestant Christian church in the Nordic countries.

Birgitta's searching and that of another couple: Raïssa and Jacques Maritain.

What is it, then, that would lead these two people on their path into the Catholic Church? In an animated way, Ulf and Birgitta describe those people—both heavenly friends, most especially the Virgin Mary, and those who are still living here on earth—and those truths which drove them forward on their journey. In many respects, their time together in the Holy Land was very decisive. It was also there, in fact, that I met Ulf Ekman for the first time, and at Notre Dame, the Vatican's center in Jerusalem. It is perhaps not so unusual that in the very land where Jesus lived, and where everything speaks of the full Christian tradition, the Catholic faith can be found. At the same time, everyone who visits this land also knows that one encounters weakness and division there in all their stark reality. Even this is a part of the comprehensive Catholic view. God does not abandon his Church. However much we Catholics do to cause the weakness and division by our sin and failures, the Lord does not allow us to darken the Church's truth and inner beauty. But one really needs a deep faith to accept that! In the Holy Land, the deep continuity and unity with our roots in the Old Covenant are also clear. This is also an integrated part of Tradition with a capital T, and when one begins to accept this fact of our faith, then one is really a good way into the Catholic reality.

Step by step, the Ekman spouses continued their journey of discovery into Catholicism. The dialogue between them about all of this is one of the most important messages of this book to our individualistic age. We are so used to the individual person always being the measuring stick. At the same time as we long for communion in the deepest part of our being, we are often fixed on ourselves. The communal search for truth as dialogue with another person is something classic in Christian tradition. We need only think of the disputations of the Middle Ages. But in the world of today, we have often lost this perspective. That is why it is so exciting to see how Ulf and Birgitta juggled their discoveries in the Catholic Church between themselves: sacraments, Mary, the pope. Just this part of the process was certainly decisive. I believe that many seekers remain standing halfway just because they have no one with whom to dialogue. Faith grows in community. We are created in the image of the Triune God, and our way into the fullness of the faith is not only an individual thing; one does not discover the communion of the Church only on one's own. Here we truly see that together it is possible to grow in the communion of the Church.

What, then, is to be done when one realizes that he truly believes the Catholic faith is the full truth that Jesus has left to his Church? Well, according to Catholic belief, one then has the duty to take the step into full, visible communion with the Catholic Church. Faith is a question of truth and salvation. One of the strictest statements of the Second Vatican Council confirms this: "Whosoever, therefore, knowing that the Catholic Church was made necessary by Christ, would refuse to enter or to remain in it, could not be saved."[2] Here many usually react strongly; it does not sound at all ecumenical or tolerant. Nevertheless, it is an uncompromising demand that the person who has truly discovered and understood that God has instituted the Catholic Church for the sake of our salvation and entrusted her

---

[2] Second Vatican Council, Dogmatic Constitution on the Church *Lumen Gentium*, November 21, 1964, chap. 1, "The Mystery of the Church", no. 14. Translation taken from the Vatican website.

with the mission of proclaiming and preserving the full truth of revelation must also belong to her. It is actually an obvious fact for every logical, thinking person. Nevertheless, this point is very difficult for our relativistic and supposedly tolerant age to accept. For the one who wishes to become Catholic, it is an indispensable condition to realize this. One does not become Catholic for emotional reasons, because of the beautiful liturgy or because there are many wonderful saints or a beautiful spirituality. These may attract one to the Church, but in the end, the decision comes down to the question of truth and salvation. When one has realized this, then and only then is the time ripe for being received into the fullness of the Catholic communion. Birgitta and Ulf realized this, and for this reason they also had to take that step, even though, in reality, everything in their lives and the atmosphere in which they lived spoke against this.

At the same time, it is difficult for many to see that the Catholic Church places great importance on ecumenism. They think it points rather to self-righteousness and a lack of humility for the Church to assert that the fullness of truth and salvation have been, in a unique way, entrusted to her and her guardianship. But this also means that the Church wants to grow in a unity of love with those who, to a greater or lesser degree, have a part of the same truth and are called to the same salvation. We, as Catholics, truly rejoice over all that unites us with other churches and denominations. The one who becomes Catholic should not do so because of a discontent with his former denomination. It is a part of the conversion process to reconcile with and be thankful to the church in which one received baptism and was able to receive so much of the Christian faith. A convert who speaks ill of or looks down upon his former denomination has not yet taken the complete step into the Catholic unity, and

there is a risk that he will sooner or later remain fixed in the
same negative attitude toward the church that he has joined.
That does not mean that one is blind to what is lacking in
the non-Catholic denominations, but how could these have
and communicate everything when they have broken away
from full unity? Instead, we rejoice over all that is true and
genuine that can, in fact, be found in these denominations.
This attitude also becomes clear in this book. Perhaps some
readers were expecting, or even hoping, for some critical
and hard words toward the Word of Life congregation. But
oh, how they were mistaken! Here we see that Ulf and Birgitta have also truly made the Catholic view of ecumenism
their own. With gratitude, they look back upon all the good
they received from Word of Life. It is not their task to chas-
tise or interrogate their former congregation. I believe that
this has also been understood by the members of Word of
Life. It made a great impression on me that so many leaders
from Word of Life wanted to be present when Birgitta and
Ulf were received into full communion with the Church in
the chapel of the Brigittine Sisters in Djursholm.

As a convert to the Catholic Church, one is able to participate in the fullness of the faith that she guards and preserves;
for the one who is received, this is so often the first and
most overwhelming impression. But one also brings something from his previous denomination that he can share with
others. That can often be forgotten along the way. For this
reason, I believe it is of the greatest importance to look a
little closer at this part of it. On the more global plane, we
have seen that the Catholic Church and the denominations
that are more Pentecostal in nature are coming closer to each
other. As with every dialogue, it is always a question of a
mutual giving and taking. What is it that we as Catholics can
receive from these denominations? On the worldwide scale,

we see that countless Catholics, not only in Latin America, but also in Europe, are going over to these more Pentecostal and charismatic congregations. They obviously find something there that they are missing with us, often something that we ourselves have forgotten or have neglected to develop: a more personal relationship with Jesus, dedication and zeal for the missions, a more biblical preaching and depth, more participation of the laity, a longing for the gifts of the Spirit. One notices that for some Catholics, Ulf's and Birgitta's conversion leads one to think more about this need within the Church. In fact, invitations have come to our two new Catholics from different parts of the world where this conversion has attracted even greater attention and interest than in Sweden—for example, in Kazakhstan and Ethiopia. This more prophetic and charismatic element of our faith needs to be strengthened in different ways. It is surely in the plan of Divine Providence for us, and thus also our responsibility as Catholics, to be obedient and clearsighted, so that we can follow the Spirit's inspirations and impulses.

The Feast of the Transfiguration
August 6, 2015

Foreword to the
English Edition

Swedish Charismatics — Catholic Converts. That could have been a subtitle of this autobiographical book that tells the stages of Ulf and Birgitta Ekman's discovery of Catholicism. Let's unpack each of its words.

Swedish: Sweden. Socialist. Sexy. Secular. A number of associations conjured up by "Sweden" in English-speaking minds are true only in a qualified sense, leaving ample room for paradox. For instance, while Sweden did make a short-lived attempt at socialism in the 1970s, it has remained what it was at heart, a free-market economy; in fact, hardcore socialism faded away in the face of popular protests. Sweden, too, does have a lot of sex appeal, but more of the apple-fresh than decadent variety. "Land of *lagom*" is a frequent designation among Sweden's own denizens for their native country, *lagom* being Swedish for "just enough and no more than that", an adverb capturing the inbred sense of moderation in Swedish culture. Wild excesses, no thank you. If ever libertine, never more than *lagom* libertine.

But is Sweden not what we call secular or secularized? Yes, it is indeed secular, like many other contemporary nations within the European cultural sphere, probably more so than most. Only a small portion of its now ten-million-strong population regularly attends religious services, and relatively few people express a firm belief in any of the organized churches of Christianity or any other religions. Yet right up to the start of the third millennium, Sweden remained a confessional state. Even now the Lutheran "Church of Sweden" retains a special position in Swedish law. A large majority of Swedish citizens are baptized Lutherans, and many of those are also confirmed in the Church of Sweden. Many Christian holidays are work-free, including the day after Christmas, the day after Easter, Good Friday, Ascension Thursday, and others. Though more a testimony to the Swedish enthusiasm for vacation, still the Christian holidays haunt the collective memory on a regular basis. Medieval churches are kept in good condition. A sense of having been a Christian country, even, in fact, of once having been Catholic, remains and is not yet forgotten. One example of this was the lively interest shown both in the visit of John Paul II to Sweden in June 1989 and the recent visit of Pope Francis in November 2016. Another is the continued interest shown in Saint Birgitta (Bridget) of Sweden, also married to an Ulf. Accounts of her life, translations of her works, even novels and plays about her have been produced in recent years, a fact that, as the reader will discover, had its role to play in the discovery of the Catholic Church by Ulf and Birgitta Ekman.

Walk into a Swedish Lutheran church, especially any of the older ones from the medieval or baroque periods, though not only these, and you will immediately notice the difference between Swedish Lutheranism and the hardcore version of Germany. Some of the best-known churches will strike the visitor as Catholic-like with their frescoes, paintings, candles lit in prayer, and even statues of the Blessed Virgin. The Church of Sweden is *lagom* Lutheran, although Swedish citizens could first legally convert to Catholicism only in 1873, and freedom of religion was first inscribed in Swedish law in 1951.

Charismatic. While free churches, that is, Protestant denominations other than the Church of Sweden, had already arisen in the first half of the nineteenth century, Swedish immigrants in the United States began to export other forms of religious experience back to Sweden by the late nineteenth century, and it is there we find the beginnings of the Pentecostalist movement in the early twentieth century. One unexpected development in Swedish religion of recent years has been the interest among a number of Swedish charismatics and Pentecostals in early Church history and the Fathers of the Church; another has been their collaboration with Catholics in a number of different contexts, collaborations such as that of the Catholic bishop of Stockholm, Anders Arborelius, the author of the foreword to the present book, himself a convert, with Sven Gunnar Hedin, the pastor of the largest Pentecostal congregation in Stockholm.

Catholic. The word "catholic" has from the start signified wholeness, not only "universality" but, more accurately, "unity in universality". As founders of a charismatic movement, one, moreover that expanded quickly and successfully in the spotlight of the secularized Swedish media, Ulf and Birgitta had to grapple with practical issues of unity, succession, and organization. The development of their charismatic congregation illustrates the need for a solid ecclesiology even within "disorganized" religion. This need is part of the explanation of what began to draw the once "anti-Catholic" Ulf himself ever closer toward Catholicism.

Converts. Some people may shudder: "Oh, another conversion story." As though "conversion stories" were all alike! From Augustine's *Confessions* to John Henry Newman's *Apologia Pro Vita Sua*, from Thomas Merton's *The Seven-Storey Mountain* to last year's *Night's Bright Darkness* by Sally Read, as well as in this very book, we are dealing with firsthand accounts of spiritual and theological discoveries. People who shy away from thoughtful and soul-searching autobiographies, such as the present one, are denying themselves important knowledge of the full richness of human experience. Others there are who may object to the very word "convert" for someone developing from a Protestant charismatic into Roman Catholic, and to these I say: please read on and give the book a chance.

I have used the plurals *charismatics* and *converts* in my proposed subtitle for this book because it contains not one but two conversion stories, intimately intertwined with each other, a married couple making the journey to Rome together. The story of Ulf and Birgitta Ekman offers unexpected glimpses into contemporary Sweden. Ulf Ekman combines Swedish secularism, Lutheranism, and American-style charismatic faith in his life story. Growing up in a secularized working class, he found faith in Christ as a young man and became both an ordained Lutheran pastor and the founder of a very well-known, fast-growing charismatic movement known as Livets Ord (Word of Life). Apart from Livets Ord's own community centered in Uppsala, the spiritual capital of Sweden, with over three thousand members, Ulf went on to found a string of other congregations, with notable success in Eastern Europe, not least in Russia itself. Birgitta, daughter of Swedish missionaries in India, whose family background was ecumenical in the sense of being both Church of Sweden and "free church", was not only Ulf's partner in marriage but also his closest collaborator in his pastoral work. For many of us who, over the years, observed their journey from prosperity Pentecostalism toward Roman Catholicism in the midst of a secularized Swedish society—for it was observable from the outside, given the Ekmans' position of leadership of a very public congregation that had inspired schools, newspapers, even a right-to-life political lobby—their story was and remains truly remarkable.

Perhaps this story of Catholic converts in secularized Sweden will be seen as particularly attractive to already believing Catholics, but I would rather hope that Ulf and Birgitta Ekman's Protestant brethren will also read it, for it shows a pastor and his wife grappling with very real problems of ecclesiology, theological misunderstandings, sacramental longing, and the urgent call to Christian unity.

DENIS SEARBY
Professor of Ancient Greek,
Stockholm University

Preface

Dear Reader!

In this book, we tell the story of a very long journey, our journey of coming close to and finally entering the Catholic Church. We tell of our own personal experiences and of events we shared together along the way. We both tell it from our own perspective.

It has been wonderful to be able to write this book together. It is a book that touches on one of the most important decisions we have made together, namely, our decision to become Catholics. We have always worked together, not least of all when it comes to writing. This collaboration suits us very well; it is so good to be able to discuss things with each other, check up on facts, and in particular dare to critique each other respectfully.

We describe the years leading up to our decision, years that were intense and filled with hard work in our non-denominational church and its far-reaching missions. The years were very rich and filled with wonderful experiences, but in this book we have concentrated primarily on what finally led us into the Catholic faith.

The chapters that are a little more theological are not an exhaustive study of theological viewpoints. We describe briefly those subjects that interested and challenged us and were decisive in our choice, but we do not give a complete apologetic account of all the reasons for these viewpoints.

We hope that this book can be beneficial to both Catholics and Protestants. To you who are Protestants, we want to say that we hope you will have an open mind and a curiosity about how Catholics actually see their faith and their Church—as we eventually did. To the Catholic reader, we wish to say that we hope you will find it interesting to see how two Protestant leaders could make this journey into the Catholic Church.

Most of all, we hope that this book will give joy and encouragement to every reader and that it in some way will lead to an increased love for Jesus Christ and to a discovery and renewed appreciation of the beauty of his Church.

Warm thanks to the publishing company Catholica and Sara Fredestad for the possibility of publishing our story and for important suggestions that have helped to make this book possible.

ULF AND BIRGITTA EKMAN
Uppsala
Feast of the Conversion of Saint Paul
January 25, 2018

Chapter 1

Ulf: Catholic Fragments
in the Background

I found myself in the office of the president-elect of Albania, Sali Berisha. It was April 1992, and, for the second time in a short period, I was visiting Albania.

My first visit had occurred the previous year in September 1991. I had then been a part of something unbelievable. I was the pastor of Word of Life, a large Swedish nondenominational church with extensive missions work in the former USSR. We had received permission from the Communist regime to present a "cultural exchange", which consisted of a large, public Christian meeting at the Tirana stadium. The Swedish pop singer Carola Häggkvist, who had just won the Eurovision Song Contest, came with us together with the large choir of Word of Life, and I had the fantastic opportunity to preach the Gospel of Jesus to an audience of about twenty thousand people. After hard negotiations, we had obtained permission to broadcast our program for two hours to the whole nation via state-controlled Albanian television. It was the first time anything like this had happened in that rigorously Communist nation.

The stadium meeting in Tirana was a powerful and very overwhelming experience for me. But the event also shook up thousands of people around Albania, who were for the first time able to hear openly and publicly about Jesus Christ. Many of them opened their hearts to Jesus and decided to follow him. For many years after this, I was able to hear testimonies about what had happened that evening at the Tirana stadium and in front of television sets around the country.

Now we had returned to Albania, where the Communist regime had just fallen. With me in the office of the president-to-be was his happy, elderly secretary. I could see that he was very eager to speak to me. He was tall and thin, a gray old man, dressed in clothes that were marked by the impoverishment behind the Iron Curtain. He came up to me and said cheerfully, in broken English: "I am also a Catholic." It was obvious that he was elated to meet a brother in the faith. I was surprised by his words but also by his radiant joy.

For the secretary, religious freedom was already a fact; he had survived the long tyranny of a brutal regime. Many others never saw freedom come. Instead, they were murdered or languished in prison under the oppression of Communism. This tough regime had even criminalized the utterance of Jesus' name and had bragged about being the world's first atheistic country.

My reaction to the elderly Catholic's joyful greeting had to do with something else, however. Great parts of Church history passed before my mind's eye in a flash. I was, of course, Protestant, not Catholic, and I did not know how to answer him. Lutheranism, Methodists, Baptists, Pentecostals, the charismatic movements, and faith movements —all of these different variations of Christendom quickly fluttered past me, and I saw myself as though sitting farthest out on a small branch, high up in a large tree. There I was,

swaying a little in the wind, engaged in some internal con-
troversy about the different ways of speaking in tongues. It
felt very curious.

I realized how impossible it was to explain all of this to
the man in front of me. How would I be able to make clear
that I was, in fact, not a Catholic, but from an organization
called Word of Life? The division of the Church stood out
suddenly in all its concrete reality. Within a fraction of a
second, I saw that right in the midst of our successful missionary work, I found myself far out on the edge of the
Christian Church. I was also a part of the tragic division in
the Body of Christ. So I smiled back, a little embarrassed,
looked him in the eyes, and said only: "Oh, that's wonderful, brother!" It felt impossible to say anything else.

From that moment—yes, precisely that moment—something began to gnaw at me, which never really let go of me,
and it had to do with the Catholic Church. I am convinced
that just this very unexpected experience was the initial moment that shook me up, woke me up, and then led me, step
by step, into full communion with the Catholic Church.
But it would take twenty-two years before the seed that he
had planted would grow into maturity.

What, then, did my experience and contact with the Catholic Church consist of during the years before this event?
When I look back, the Catholic Church was largely absent
from my awareness. Raised as I was in a secularized working-
class environment in Gothenburg, I simply never came into
contact with Catholics and hardly any other Christians, either. Nor was the Catholic faith something to which I gave
any thought.

I remember a few photos in a history textbook repre-
senting the place of pilgrimage in Lourdes. I also vaguely
remember the Second Vatican Council, a few popes who

were briefly mentioned on television, and pictures of Pope John XXIII, who inaugurated the council. I remember one teacher's critical comments in a few religion classes. Her remarks for the most part concerned the Catholic view of sexuality and criticized the fact that in the modern world there existed such people who did not understand the advantages of contraception, which for secularized Swedes was so incomprehensible. In 1968, Pope Paul VI made a pronouncement against contraceptives, and the attacks on him spread like wildfire throughout the media of the Western world. In my left-leaning world in Gothenburg, there was hardly anyone who wanted to, or could, understand the pope's view.

I remember very well a single spontaneous visit with a friend to Christ the King Catholic church in Gothenburg at the end of the 1960s. It was a gloomy afternoon when we did not have anything else to do. We looked in cautiously and were surprised by a friendly woman, who kindly and thoroughly explained to us what it was we saw before us near the altar. After a while we had had enough, and we moved toward the exit and disappeared. In my aunt's newspaper, I read a critical article about a young Swedish man who had become a monk somewhere in Europe, and that bewildered me. How could anyone understand such a curious decision to leave everything exciting in this world in order to bury himself in a monastery?

Yes, that was surely the extent of my fragmented impressions of the Catholic Church when I was growing up. My mother had grown up in a Lutheran family, and she had a deep sense of Christianity. Her father had been a church-warden and was a deeply religious man. My father was critical of institutional faith and was quick to discuss scandals in the Lutheran Church. Still, they had me baptized as an infant, like most Swedes did in those days. Early on in school I received good impressions of the faith through teachers. So I was quite open until my Lutheran confirmation at the age of fifteen. The rest of my teenage years were quite restless, and gradually I became more critical, though I could never call myself an atheist.

In that sense, I was surely like most secular young people in the 1960s—without knowledge, uninterested, and prejudiced in general. I was that way toward most things that had to do with the Christian faith. I understood Christianity to be something outdated, conservative, and superstitious, and the Catholic faith, which for centuries had been banned in Sweden, seemed so strange to me—outside my view, beyond my horizons, unknown, foreign, and a little frightening.

~

But then, at the end of May 1970, Jesus came into my life. I had a friend who suddenly became a Christian, which really surprised me. The change in his life profoundly influenced me, and I often avoided him because he now made me nervous. But one day I was in his apartment, and he asked if he could pray for me. As he started to pray, I felt terribly uncomfortable and ran out the door. On my way home, in the trolley, inside of me I heard the words "Your sins can be forgiven" over and over again. A deep sense of conviction came over me. I realized only Jesus could help me. When I came home to my room, I knelt down and asked Jesus to forgive me of my sins and to be my Lord and Savior. From that day on, I called myself a Christian.

That summer was a revolutionary, wonderful, and intense time. I discovered and got to know Jesus personally. With my faith in him, my life received a new beginning, and I

wanted to follow him. Everything changed in me to the
very foundation of my being. Becoming a Christian was so
radically different from how I had perceived it before, and it
really felt like coming home. It answered something in the
depths of my being. God's love was so tangibly close and
concrete in my life that I could not resist it. The old was
truly gone, and something completely new had begun.

From this, I came to terms with different digressions of
my teenage years and the spirit of the late sixties, the leftist movement, and the hippie wave of which I had been a
part for some years. It felt as though the different, disparate
parts of my life, my interests and talents, now finally fit together as a whole. Suddenly life had a real meaning, a context with both value and a function. To be whole, to be a
human being, to come home and be a child of God because
of Christ, in Christ, and with Christ was in fact an overwhelming experience of God's grace. It was an experience
that transformed and then carried me through all the years.
Joy and security in God were the fundamental feelings that
ran through me, and since then these feelings have followed
me throughout my life.

The faith I found at that time had a breadth to it in
which Christians from many denominations came together,
prayed, read the Bible, and evangelized. Most were warm,
free-church believers who had fellowship beyond denominational borders. There were elements of everything from
the Lutheran State Church, the Church of Sweden, to the
new charismatic movement, which at that time welled forth
like a flood over the world. It was a new and exciting world
for me, the existence of which I could not even have imagined just a few months before. This new world opened up
for me when I opened myself to Christ.

My Christian life continued during my university studies

in Uppsala. It was at the beginning of the 1970s, when many young Christians did not care very much about the denominations. The most important thing was that you loved Jesus. Naturally, it was not like this everywhere in Swedish Christianity, but this was the warm, spiritual environment into which I came, and for this I am very grateful. In my free time, I was completely occupied with student evangelization and Bible studies in an evangelical student organization called the Navigators. This gave me stability, direction, discipline, and roots in my Christian life. The Bible became a living and totally fascinating book that I read (and continue to read) daily.

After completing a bachelor's degree in philosophy, I began to study theology. The thought of becoming a priest in the Lutheran Church of Sweden began to grow in me seriously. I did not really notice it, but, step-by-step, the Catholic Church also came a little closer. There were a few of us theology students who made a student visit to the Catholic parish of Saint Lars in Uppsala. It was interesting though still a little foreign even though I was now a Christian. In my background, I did not have any deep grounding in the Swedish church, either. Even though certain parts of the liturgy spoke to me, it still felt a little too rigid and formal. I was simply not used to going to a liturgical church, and with my evangelizing, outgoing, more free-church emphasis on the Christian life, I presumptuously thought that the liturgy was unnecessary and stifling.

After a few years, some friends began to take me to Saint Ansgar, a "high-church" Lutheran church that many students attended. It was there that I began, more and more, to understand, appreciate, and enter into the Mass, with its rich meaning. But, although I never drew any further conclusions from this, a few friends did, so that for them it became a stepping-stone into the Catholic Church. I myself, however, was far too influenced by evangelicalism and the charismatic movement to allow these inspirations to affect me. I preferred rather to be out evangelizing, telling students about Jesus, explaining and defending the Gospel, and at the same time associating and praying with others in prayer groups.

At regular intervals, however, I visited Koinonia, a Lutheran high-church student community where mass was celebrated regularly. It was very open to the Catholic Church. Out of this group came a Lutheran monastery in Östanbäck with a number of Lutheran monks who followed the Benedictine Rule. I had great respect for Caesarius Cavallin, one of my teachers who was now the abbot of this little monastery, but I never went out to see them during my years at the university. Different Catholic impulses were coming from all directions, but I could neither understand nor respond to them.

In my theological studies, I sometimes came in contact with Catholic teaching of high quality. We studied Joseph Ratzinger's *Introduction to Christianity*, and I profited greatly from it, and alongside of that, I read, among other things, Gunnel Vallquist's four diaries from the Second Vatican Council, which was held from 1962 to 1965. It was captivating literature, but it served more as spiritual orientation and general education for me than as a direct guide. Nevertheless, the knowledge of this council, which was so revolutionary, was like a seed within me that would one day begin to bear fruit.

At Easter 1976, I went along with a friend on a trip to Rome, where we spent a week walking and taking in the sights. We could not afford to do many of the daily excursions that cost extra, and we mostly looked around ourselves. Nevertheless, it was a very enriching trip. The climax was Easter night, when we succeeded in getting seats inside Saint Peter's Basilica. I could hardly believe my eyes when I saw the enthusiasm of the people as Pope Paul VI was carried in, sitting on a high throne (*sedia gestatoria*). The nuns completely exploded with joy, and the jubilation reached the ceiling of the entire church. I myself remembered that this was the pope who had spoken out against contraception in 1968 and was so hated for it. It was something totally different to see him now, so close to me, and to be able to experience the peoples' great love for him instead of the aggressive, leftist attacks I had heard. Yet he looked tired. He was sick and did not live very much longer, but he sat there patiently and waved so kindly to all. It made a strong impression on me. Unfortunately, we had to leave early in order to make it back in time to the hotel before they locked the door. We went out when the great bells resounded over Saint Peter's Square. We were sorry to have to leave just then.

For several years I had been praying about a wife. After six years of being single during my years at Uppsala University, I was really ready for her to show up. One day not long after I returned from Rome, a priest asked me to join him on one of his retreats. During a Bible study about the Holy Spirit, some guests appeared; one of them immediately caught my attention. This was Birgitta. Later, we took a walk and discovered our mutual interests and goals. She was beautiful, kind, and intelligent, and she loved the Lord. I fell in love, head over heels. In December of that same year, 1976, we got married, and I was so happy.

In my spiritual life, the low church and the charismatic expression of the faith gradually assumed an ever-greater place. I had started to sense strongly that I was to seek to be ordained as a priest in the Swedish Lutheran Church. Birgitta and I prayed about it and felt it was God's call. I enthusiastically prepared myself for a life as a minister and longed to preach and teach the Word of God and evangelize in a secular society. In January 1979, I was ordained a Lutheran priest by Bishop Bertil Gärtner in the diocese of Gothenburg and was assigned as a student chaplain in an evangelical Lutheran student movement in Uppsala. Sometimes I came in brief contact with my colleague, the Catholic chaplain. He was very friendly, but since we lived in different worlds, we did not actually have any direct theological exchanges. I also, of course, shared the common Lutheran and charismatic opinions and prejudices about Catholicism. To a great extent, I was unaware of the more universal Church and the ecumenical, theological discussions at that time.

Besides the obligatory reading of theological textbooks during my study years, I also read a bit of Pentecostal-charismatic literature, which was circulating among the theology students. Even though some called them "lightweight theology", these books were, in fact, refreshing and spiritually uplifting. Reading them was a change from the more sterile, academic, and quite liberal theology at the University of Uppsala. This literature mainly described the work of the Holy Spirit in a person's life. But an anti-Catholic position had frequently crept into the often-fantastic experiences and missionary adventures described there. Many of the stories and experiences dealt with people who had come out of a nominal, more formal religious background, often from Catholic countries, and arrived at "a more living and personal faith". For the authors, it was often obvious that Catholics needed to be converted and could hardly be considered real Christians. The Catholic Church was seen as a rigid giant, old and out of step with the times, which was against new movements and dismissive of a personal Christian life. She was looked upon as a more or less dead church or, in more blunt phrasing, as the whore of Babylon in the Book of Revelation. Here the interpretations could vary, but common to the free-church literature I read was a strong criticism and a clear repudiation of all things Catholic.

This repudiation stemmed from a strong theological undercurrent not only from certain free churches, but perhaps even more so from the low church and Bible-centered Lutheranism. All of this gradually influenced my view of the Catholic Church, which became increasingly negative during that time. To check the facts in order to see if these claims were really true, to compare them with what Catholics themselves said about their faith and their spiritual life, or to read Catholic spiritual literature was simply not on the agenda. I remember, nevertheless, that at the Christian bookstore in Uppsala, among all the charismatic literature, there was also Carmelite literature by Saint John of the Cross and Saint Teresa of Avila. I had my office in this bookstore, and I remember how curious I was about these books. I felt an inner drawing to read them, but I did not. The impression of these books remained, however, and I continued to feel a quiet inner prompting to read them.

But I was drawn more and more to Pentecostal-charismatic Christianity at that time, with its fresh emphasis on the life and gifts of the Spirit in the ordinary Christian's life. At the same time, I was skeptical of an all too liberally influenced and academically dry and intellectualized faith, on the one hand, and an all too leftist, politicized, secularly oriented faith, on the other, where the horizontal seemed to eliminate completely the vertical aspect of the faith.

I thought that both these positions relativized and distorted the faith. They seemed to dismantle the classical dogmas and doctrinal concepts while treating the Scriptures subjectively and individualistically. For me, the vitally important elements of the faith were: a personal love for Jesus, obedience to him, faithfulness to the Scriptures and the classical dogmas, and openness to the charismatic life. This was what I had been brought into when I became a professed Christian, and it was this that I had since become familiar with and learned to love. I could not imagine compromising on any of these elements. I had learned from Luther about "adiafora", that there are things unessential, peripheral, and not necessary for salvation, and, in an all too evangelical way, I accepted that much in the history of the Church was in fact a superstructure, unnecessary theological rubbish, which hid the simplicity and power of the Gospel.

The more I came into the charismatic life, which, I must say really had many positive sides, the more critical I became of the liberal theology of the traditional Lutheran Church. That which I understood to be just empty façades in different outward forms I perceived mostly as an obstacle to the growth of faith in people's lives. I had no idea how much I would be properly challenged on these very points later on. Nor did I realize how many prejudices lay in these so-called "truths".

My years as a student chaplain in Uppsala were very rewarding. At the same time, I was drawn to the mission field, and I had an ever-stronger desire to be a missionary. I shared this desire with Birgitta. She had been born and raised in India, where her parents were Methodist missionaries, so she had received the missionary spirit in the cradle, so to speak. We were both completely prepared for a life in the Lord's service, but after a couple of years, the possibility opened up for me to study for a year at a charismatic Bible school, Rhema, in Oklahoma. I finished my work as a student chaplain in Uppsala, and we moved to Tulsa. By this time, we were a small family, and it was quite an adventure for our boys to spend a year in the United States. It was fun to hear the little ones use some English words when they played with their new friends. That year influenced us in many ways. I saw the pragmatic ways in which Americans passionately reached out with the Gospel and how new congregations got started and then apparently saw quick growth.

This was something new for me. My desire was, of course, to instruct and equip laymen, ordinary believers, in the Word of God, the personal life of faith, and the life of the Spirit. I wanted to mobilize them for evangelization and mission. During this year in the United States, I received much inspiration for this. It was a great time. Incidentally, I do not think I met a single Catholic during that whole year.

Our time in the United States did not change my critical attitude toward the historical churches but rather strengthened it, and this attitude continued to follow me. Because of the liberal, theological position toward the Bible and the classical dogmas that I saw in the Swedish church, I thought there was justification for this critique. But the criticism was in certain areas rather exaggerated and generalized. Above all, my critique was built on an ecclesiologically weak foundation. It was a foundation that I shared in principle with all low-church and free-church views. In it, there was a great lack of awareness and disregard for what God had done throughout Church history. There was also a somewhat naïve idea that we, by going back to the first community of Christianity found in the Acts of the Apostles, could merely jump over two thousand years of Church history in order to find the origin, the original Christianity, and just begin from there. It was like looking for the roots but ignoring the tree that had grown up from them. The idea we had was that the tree had more or less detached itself from the roots.

This view of the Church was based on the fact that new

movements were constantly emerging out of the old churches that had turned antiquated and rigid. We thought this was a natural phenomenon led by the Spirit. It was something like streams that must break off into new channels in order to be able to reach their goal. For the most part, we saw the historical Church as an obstacle to a healthy spiritual life.

I would later be forced to reconsider properly the position I held in regard to this weak and erroneous ecclesiological perspective. I had not yet reflected on the fact that Jesus is not truly Jesus in the fullest sense without the Church, his visible Body. I was, in an individualistic way, so focused on the personal Christian life, and the individual person's service to God, that, for me, the Church was not much more than the individual congregation to which one belonged. It was, in its own way, rather loosely united with other free congregations. The focus lay mainly on the individual Christian's own relationship with Jesus. The congregation, the Church, came in second or third place.

Home again from the United States in 1982, I was completely prepared to start a Bible school for Christians from all denominations. However, I was uncertain in the beginning about the idea of starting new congregations. Both Birgitta and I thought it sounded a little too foreign. I cannot claim that there were any deeper ecclesiological convictions underlying the fact that we, in the end, nevertheless did take the step and started the Word of Life church in Uppsala in May 1983.

At this time, there were hardly any new, independent churches in Sweden, so when we established our church, it created quite a stir in the media and naturally a friction within the Church of Sweden. The archbishop summoned me to his office and demanded that I choose—either remain a Lutheran minister or continue the work with Word of Life and lose my ordination. We had a good and polite talk, and I understood his position. But I had already made up my mind. I chose to continue with the Word of Life church and Bible school and thus resigned as a Lutheran minister but remained a member of the Church of Sweden.

We saw that our Bible school students needed a daily community life and a church to attend on Sundays. I threw myself into the many tasks and experienced great satisfaction in all of this, despite the fact that there were many external difficulties. The Bible school and the congregation grew quickly. We saw a great hunger for God's Word, and both the young and the old from many denominations poured into the Bible school in Uppsala. We sent out teams to evangelize in both Sweden and Asia. Over the years, there were over six thousand people who were sent out in different teams.

When the Iron Curtain fell in 1989, a unique and fantastic time followed for us. It was a time of passionate mission work and founding congregations in many nations but, above all, in Russia and the old Soviet satellite countries. We worked according to the Pentecostal-charismatic model. Hundreds of congregations sprang up in these different countries, and many of them had thousands of members. We started Bible schools in many places, and, over the course of the years, we saw over fifty thousand students attending these schools for at least one year. It gave us a deep satisfaction to see so many thousands of people change from a life of atheistic emptiness to a life of loving and following Jesus. I myself, and others with me, frequently shuttled back and forth, in and out of Russia. These were incredibly intensive and rewarding years.

But it was also very inspiring to build a local congregation in Uppsala and to help people deepen their faith. We wanted them to have courage in their service to the Lord, to find their place, and to be active and outgoing in sharing the Gospel and serving their neighbors.

The congregation in Uppsala grew, and bit-by-bit we started many different activities. Besides evangelization and mission, Christian school and media activities developed. Over the years came more of both spiritual guidance and theological education. We built a very large church hall, seating four thousand, which was dedicated in the summer of 1987. These were great undertakings that demanded much of our strength and energy, but they were exciting times. Sometimes we had no idea how the financial resources would materialize for all of this, but we constantly saw God's help and proceeded step by step with his grace through all the challenges. At that time, I was so focused that I had almost no time to see what was happening outside the horizons of our own congregation. There were, however, a few exceptions.

One of these exceptions was that, in June 1989, during a period of great intensity, Pope John Paul II came to Sweden. It was naturally a great event for the Church, because it was the first time a pope had visited Sweden and the Nordic countries. In Denmark and Norway, his reception was cooler than in Sweden. His visit was even met with protests by bishops. In Sweden, the pope received a warm welcome from the Swedish church. Some of the free churches were skeptical, however, and we ourselves were negative. As I mentioned, I had been influenced by anti-Catholic literature, mostly of the American fundamentalist kind, and several of our Bible instructors were of the same persuasion. Unfortunately, through this influence, our defense of the truth of the Gospel also became a public opposition to Catholicism. I wrote two negative articles, and in one of them I was very critical of the pope's visit to Uppsala.

The day before his arrival, I organized a prayer meeting with our congregation at Old Uppsala on top of the Viking burial mounds. The pope was to celebrate Mass in Old Uppsala just next to these mounds, and we prayed for God's protection during this papal visit. We were "against" a return of Catholicism in Sweden, and we prayed that nothing more than God's pure and unadulterated Word would be proclaimed and that the evangelical faith would be preserved in this country. We were a couple of hundred people together, combining this prayer meeting with a picnic. Our prayers were fervent but not aggressive or hateful.

Even if we were honest in our intention, this behavior was very offensive to those Catholics who heard about it. When I look back today on this episode and other occasions when I was negative toward the Catholic Church, I obviously feel regret. Thanks be to God, actions such as these were not regular behavior but receded more and more into the background when our attention was focused on so many other things. Despite all, we wanted to have a positive basis for our preaching, not a negative one.

Fear of Catholicism still exists today in parts of the free churches, and in Pentecostal-charismatic spirituality, I am now exposed to it myself at times. The critical attitude toward the Catholic Church stayed with me for many years, but I must nevertheless say that it was not a primary, driving, or dominating factor in my Christian life. It was, however, still a part of my general understanding of the faith at that time, and I accepted those prejudices which flourish in the part of Christianity to which I belonged.

In a book that I found many years later, I read the pope's homily at the Mass in Old Uppsala, and I was struck by how his preaching actually was permeated by both "God's pure and unadulterated Word" and pastoral love and care. He finished very strongly by saying: "The promise is for you and your children. The Lord has been faithful to his promises. You must be faithful to him. Go forward together in faith, hope and love, alive in the Spirit of our Lord Jesus Christ. Amen." Our worry had truly been unwarranted.

Chapter 2

Ulf: The Dawn that Leads to Reevaluation

There are ecclesiological scholars who have tried to describe the different developmental stages of new revivalist movements. They are of the opinion that in the beginning, revivalist movements are often open to all of God's people, but that when they are questioned for different reasons, they close themselves in on their own group in order to survive.

As a result of this situation, they end up mustering strength within their own group in order to go out into missions. Eventually, not the least out on the mission field, revivalist movements have more and more contact with other groups that carry out similar activities and are then forced to relate to them in a more open way. They face the choice of continuing to be closed and competitive toward others or opening up to more unity and collaboration. Opening up leads to an increased maturity, where one begins to accept the experiences and spirituality of others in a more affirming and inclusive way. Thereby one can gradually return to the openness that existed in the beginning, but now with a greater depth and maturity.

~

During the entire decade of the 1990s, I was very occupied with our international mission work. The Word of Life mission now reached many countries, particularly in the East. We began Bible schools and were able to open many new congregations deep inside Russia and in central Asia. The work demanded much time, strength, and resources.

At some point in the mid-nineties, I read a book by the well-known evangelical preacher Charles Colson while I was on a long flight to Australia. Colson had previously been an adviser to President Nixon, and he ended up in prison due to his involvement in the Watergate scandal. Before he received his prison sentence, he converted and became a Christian. Later, he went on to form Prison Fellowship ministries, and he became a major voice in the ecumenical movement. Now I was reading his book *The Body*, which was about the Body of Christ. Colson challenged me when he radically questioned the division in the Body of Christ and gave numerous examples of how Christians could and ought to work together beyond denominational borders. Through his book, he wanted to help Protestants become aware of the diminishment and waste of spiritual resources that result from the division in the Body of Christ. That was a message I needed to hear just then, and it helped me to realize that we Christians must strive for unity.

Reading his book gave me cause for reflection. Thoughts such as "Are we working in the right way?" and "What will the long-term result be?" began, little by little, to present themselves to me. I never doubted the necessity of evangelizing and preaching. But *how*? Were we doing it in the right way? Could it be that our preoccupation with short-term successes hindered us from seeing problems that could arise a little later on, in the long term? Were we causing an even deeper, more permanent division, and, if so, was this acceptable? Were all these missionary initiatives founded in a proper way, so that their fruit would endure? These questions were not completely formed within me, but they rose to the surface, small thoughts of hesitation and doubt. And they did not really leave me in peace.

But more often my pragmatic eagerness took over. It was not difficult to emphasize the necessity of missionary work and to point out the strong growth of our efforts. Many people came to faith in Christ. But what would happen later, after that?

After a few years of evangelism and church planting in Russia, we took the initiative to start a more organized education of pastors. This, of course, helped to establish and strengthen the pastors and their congregations. At the same time, we let the work in the former Soviet Union take a rather loose organization, open to the local churches' own initiatives, because we thought this was the guidance of the Holy Spirit. This resulted in hundreds of more or less autonomous congregations. The unity between the pastors was mostly relational, not structural.

It did not take long, however, before I began to think more seriously about the strengths and weaknesses of this understanding of what a church is. We saw examples of how disoriented some pastors could become, how unmanageable others were, and how some of them fell into heresy or unhealthy exaggerations. Given how strongly the emphasis lay on the freedom of the individual Christian, the freedom of the local congregation, and the strictly relational fellowship of the pastors, the network lacked the necessary measures of control when something began to go awry. As long as there was clear sailing, there was not so much to worry about, but when storms came, one could see how fragile and vulnerable a local church could be. This was because, in reality, when there were differences of opinion, no authority outside the local congregation was accepted,

I also began to think about the survival of these churches. How long does a movement and wave of renewal last? How long do individual congregations and movements survive? How does one transmit life, teaching, power, and essential regulations from one generation to another? Was it really right that an evangelical work should last only a short time, then fade away and make way for new movements? Where was the continuity and stability that was passed down from generation to generation? The strength of revivalist movements lies in the present moment, but the weakness lies in an unwillingness or inability to plan for and think about the long term. This began to disturb me.

I thought more and more about these and similar questions, which were relevant to the great activities we were pursuing. Reflecting on these questions did not mean that I did not appreciate the great mission work that Word of Life did during these years. We saw remarkable things in our mission work, but it became increasingly clear to me that essential foundation stones were missing.

I began to see that we had in some way backed ourselves into a corner through our criticism of what was stable, long lasting, and durable—what we considered old, rigid, and dead in the historical churches. The Pentecostal-charismatic view of the church, which stems from independent congregationalism, where the new continually replaces the old, did not seem to hold up when difficulties arose. It seemed to start out well through different, strong initiatives, but it lacked the inherent stability and continuity that is passed on through the generations. The result was, instead, division after division.

Ours was an honest search for the original, for the roots,

for the authentic congregation, and for the Gospel's real power. But when, at the same time, that search was marred by skepticism and a negative basic view of that which is enduring and from the past, it led to isolation and to strenuous attempts, time and again, to rediscover the wheel.

~

At the end of the 1990s, Birgitta and I began seriously to open our eyes to the fundamental meaning of Christian unity and its central place in the faith. Unity, as I described, was not a subject that had been emphasized in our circles. The fact was that it was mostly associated with a more liberal Christian faith, where one seemed to be willing to compromise both the Scriptures and the central dogmas of the faith. In certain free-church communities, there was a fear of organized unity and a bureaucratic superstructure that could stifle the freedom of the Spirit. So ecumenism was not particularly high on the agenda of Pentecostal-charismatics; on the contrary, it was more or less suspect. Christian unity ought to be spiritual and invisible, not external and structural, many thought.

At the same time, none of us could ignore what Jesus himself had said about unity. In the Gospel of John 17:21, Jesus says: "That they may all be one; even as you, Father, are in me, and I in you, that they also may be in us, *so that* the world may believe that you have sent me" [italics mine]. These are very strong words. It concerns a deep and intimate unity, which is at the same time so concrete and so tangible that it can really be seen and can influence the world. And the concrete, the externally visible, always has some structured form. This was Jesus' own prayer, and I began to realize that he really wanted this. Despite all the fragmentation in Christianity, it was encouraging to think that Jesus' prayers are, in fact, always heard. These words were a part of his spiritual testament to his disciples before he went to his death on the Cross. Without a doubt, these words have great weight.

It was not only these important questions but also the search for relevant answers to strengthen individual Christians, local congregations, and spiritual movements that eventually led us into contact with the Catholic Church. Where I least imagined it possible, I found answers.

It was during this time, shortly before the millennium, that I had a thought that has since never left me. It rose up from within me like an appeal, an invitation: "Learn to know the essence of the church." It was an expression that I had, in fact, not thought about at all, nor was I familiar with it. My thoughts were more occupied with the activities and "vision" of the church, its members, and its organization: its mission, prayer, praise, and evangelization. I thought I knew the breadth and the length rather well, but I thirsted for more of the height and the depth, to paraphrase Ephesians 3:18. The thought of the church's true nature, its essence—what the church actually *is* in its "personality"— had not occupied my mind at all. This new thought spurred me to reflect more deeply and in new ways. What would the consequences of all this be for our work and relationships?

A large part of my work now consisted of preaching tours in Sweden and abroad. As word spread about our work at Word of Life, I was frequently invited to charismatic churches and conferences to speak, often before thousands of people. One trip in February 1998 took us all the way to Hawaii. One early morning, while Birgitta lay sleeping, I took a walk along Waikiki beach in central Honolulu. When I had gone a bit, I decided to walk in from the shore and take one of the main streets back to the hotel. I walked and prayed silently, enjoying the early morning. Then I saw a little church, which seemed, in fact, to be open, despite the early hour. Some people went in, and I thought that there was perhaps morning prayer there, so I followed them in and sat down far in the back. To my surprise, the church was almost full. I realized that I had come into a Catholic church. At the front, on the altar, there stood something. I did not quite know what it was. Only later did I understand that it was a monstrance with a large Host.[1]

I sat in my pew and prayed quietly, the way I was accustomed to doing. Suddenly, I became overwhelmed by something I had only experienced a few times before. It was a strong experience of God's presence. It is not possible to explain it in any other way. It seemed to me that his presence penetrated deeply and filled the whole church. It was so astounding that I did not know what I would do. It came as a complete surprise. "God is, in fact, very present in this church among these Catholics", I thought with astonishment.

This sense was so overwhelming that it did not leave me for several hours, and I still remember the power of what I experienced. That morning it left within me a new conviction of God's presence in the Catholic Church. Much later, I realized that it had to do with the Divine Presence in the Blessed Sacrament, but I did not understand that at the time. But what I did understand was enough to begin to change my perception of the Catholic Church in the depths of my being.

---

[1] The monstrance (from the Latin *monstro*, to show) is an often very ornate container where one places the consecrated Host, the Communion Bread, so that it is visible for worship.

~

In October 1999, Birgitta and I traveled to Rome for a week's vacation. I had not been there since my trip as a student and thought it would be really great to go there again. We appreciated all the beauty—and, of course, the pasta, ice cream, and cappuccino. Ancient Rome with its history, going all the way back to the great era of the Roman Empire, is always fascinating, but now what began to captivate and challenge us was the Christian Rome.

On Wednesday, there was an open audience with Pope John Paul II at Saint Peter's Square, an exciting experience. The pope came riding through the masses of people in his white "popemobile". At first I thought: "It is amazing how much fanfare there is surrounding him" and felt that the people were a little too enthusiastic. We managed somehow to stand so near that the pope passed very close to us. Then Birgitta shouted joyfully and spontaneously in English: "God bless you, brother!" My first reaction was really ultra-Protestant: "How do you know that he is a brother?" But at the same time, I felt rather foolish. Of course he was a brother, despite all that I thought separated us.

A young man from Australia stood next to us in the crowd. Perhaps he noticed our little discussion because he turned around, looked at me, and asked in a friendly way who I believed the pope actually was. I answered diplomatically that he was, of course, the bishop of Rome. Then he looked at me in a serious way and said: "Is that all he is?" The question hit me with an unexpected impact. I asked him what he meant by his question. "Is he not the shepherd of the whole Church, her universal pastor?" he replied. Someone else, someone greater than that young man from Australia, spoke to me at that moment. I was totally struck and felt completely convicted, in a way I had not at all expected. What he said pricked my conscience. Could it really be true that there was an office, a pastoral ministry, that gathered, united, and served *all* Christians? The thought was so foreign to me, but, at the same time, I realized that I did not have any courage to contradict this young man. At that moment, it was he who was standing on the side of faith and I on the side of unbelief, even if I liked to call myself a preacher of the faith. The question stayed with me, and I could not shake it off the whole week. Birgitta laughed heartily at my confusion. She surely thought it was a little funny to see me, always a great talker, at a loss for words.

We went to the big Catholic bookstore near Saint Peter's Square and saw the great mass of theological literature on the shelves. I found many books that dealt with those very questions about which I myself had been thinking. So I bought a large pile of books and lay on my bed in the hotel room and read during our breaks. Birgitta also found much that interested her. A new world slowly opened up for us, and we realized that well-thought-out answers existed to the questions we had, answers that had already been formulated hundreds of years ago.

There still remained a certain suspicion in me. Could I trust these authors? How could I determine what was right and wrong? But the hunger for answers to my questions took over, and I understood that I also needed to humble myself and dare to be open and, in fact, listen to others who knew more than I did. Now a study began that would continue for fifteen years. It became important for me to hear what Catholics themselves said about their faith. Listening only to what non-Catholics claimed that Catholics believe no longer sufficed.

~

At home in Sweden, we had gradually begun to reestablish contact with the high-church movement. We attended a few lectures by Bishop Gärtner, who had ordained me in 1979. He had come to Uppsala for the annual meeting of "high-church" priests and lay people. It was very rewarding to meet with him again. The high church in Sweden was, of course, Catholic-inspired, and it was greatly criticized for its position on the priestly vocation, since it was against the ordination of women priests. At the same time, it took a kind of middle position, where one could also appear to be rather anti-Catholic. It was obvious that "conversions to Rome" were not approved of. One thought oneself to be, more or less, the true Catholic Church in Sweden. I found this a bit remarkable. But it was nice to meet these friends and exchange thoughts with them. Most of them were very kind toward us, and it felt good to be in contact again. Christian unity, as I said before, began to feel more and more important.

In December 1998, the Catholic Church had received her first Swedish bishop since the Reformation, Anders Arborelius. Both Birgitta and I were fascinated with how this new bishop expressed himself in the media. He was obviously very intelligent and spiritual and yet friendly and humorous, and we rejoiced over this man of the Spirit with his humble authority.

Two and a half years later, in August 2001, I invited him to Word of Life for a private lunch. I was so happy when he accepted, and we had a very enriching conversation. I realized that I had before me a person who would come to mean much for Christianity in all of Sweden and who would be a part of drawing up the spiritual map in Sweden.

To have this warm contact with Bishop Anders was very significant for me.

~

At Word of Life in Uppsala, the work continued at full speed. After the turn of the millennium, I began to think not only of working with missions from within Sweden, but also that Birgitta and I would perhaps go out to a mission field ourselves, settle down, and live there and work more permanently. The country we thought of was India. For some years, I had traveled frequently to India, where I had pastors' conferences in many large cities. The pastors' interest in these conferences grew, and I began to realize that if we wanted to do something more lasting, we ought not to travel in and out of the country but actually live there for a longer period of time. We prayed for clarity about God's will in this, and over time we felt great peace about this decision. So in January 2002, it happened that we left the congregation in Uppsala, and my assistant pastor took over as head pastor for a few years.

Our departure went a little differently from what we had imagined, however. We had great problems getting visas to India, so, instead, we ended up in Singapore for a few months, and from there we traveled around in the Far East. This tremendous trip took us to Malaysia, Indonesia, Hong Kong, Taiwan, New Zealand, and Fiji. I preached in many different churches and conferences throughout the trip. In the month of May, we traveled via the United States home to Sweden again in order to lead Word of Life's great annual tour to Israel. It did not feel as though we had moved back home again; rather, it felt like a layover of sorts.

~

Since 1987, I had led tours to Israel once or twice a year, and these journeys had been enormously inspiring. Our interest in Israel, both the ancient and the modern, only grew. At the same time, we came in contact with Jews from all over the former Soviet Union. Many of them had lived with secret or concealed identities. Some of them had been persecuted; some had landed in prison. There was no doubt that there was strong anti-Semitism—religiously, institutionally, and generally—among the people in Russia, and we took it as a great mission to work against it. Due to the anti-Semitism, many Jews wanted to leave Soviet Russia, despite the fact that this entailed great sacrifices and difficulties for them, and we had the possibility of helping thousands of them emigrate and return to Israel, their ancient homeland.

Through this contact with Jews—secular and religious—both in Russia and in Israel, I began to appreciate more and more of their religious traditions. I began to see and understand in a new way the suffering they had endured for so long. I realized what a sacrifice it had meant for them to try to preserve their faith in foreign lands, throughout all the centuries of persecution. It was inspiring to see their love for the *Torah*, the law, the prayers, the biblical readings, and their old traditions. We became personally acquainted with the Israeli tenor and cantor Dudu Fisher and were invited many times to his home during Sukkot, the feast of Tabernacles. In some way it was, in fact, the Jews who made me begin to understand the importance of a living tradition. I realized in a new way that the Temple service and life in the synagogue were things that Jesus himself had lived and shared with his people. He was, in fact, a Jew.

There are plenty of promises in the Old Testament of the return of the Jewish people to their ancient homeland, and their longing for the Messiah is so clearly foretold and fulfilled in Jesus of Nazareth. There was so much here that united us, while, at the same time, there were things that divided us. The Jewish faith is the womb and cradle of the Christian faith and the Church. I knew this theoretically, but I was able to experience it very practically and powerfully there in Israel.

During this summer journey to Israel with Word of Life in 2002, it became clear to us that it was here, to Jerusalem, that we should move. The way to India was closed for us, and we could only trust that God would open and close the doors that he willed. We had thought a great deal about the possibility of eventually living in Israel, sometime in the distant future. Now we actually moved there in August in order to prepare for the opening of a study center. We would also continue to be active from there in the missionary work of Word of Life in other countries. Jerusalem became our home for three years, and it was during these years that we seriously began to come in contact with a living Catholic faith.

Israel is like no other country in the world, and Jerusalem cannot be compared to any other city. For the person who stands at a distance and forms his idea only from the media reports, it is nothing but a large trouble spot with very serious conflicts that demand one take a position. But when one goes and lives there, a life that is full of spiritual riches also opens up. One truly finds oneself to be on holy ground. It is the Holy Land, and in this very place, the manger once stood where Jesus lay as a newborn baby. Here, the Word became flesh and made his dwelling among us. Here, among these mountains and hills, on these roads, Jesus walked and preached about the Kingdom of God. Here, on this ground in Jerusalem, our salvation was won and we were redeemed by the Precious Blood of Jesus. Here stood the Cross, and here was the open grave. In Israel, more than anywhere else on earth, the Christian faith becomes very concrete. Here—if one is open—one is cured of gnostic and overly spiritual elements, which tend to diminish the faith's anchoring in the physical and corporeal. It was in this environment that I began to understand the theology of the Incarnation and the sacramental faith in a deeper way.

~

The first year we lived in central Jerusalem, and we experienced the immediate closeness and deadly seriousness of the political conflicts. On two occasions, bombs exploded in our own neighborhood, both times with fatal results. The atmosphere among many Israelis was strained and tense. One could never know when or where the bombs would explode the next time. Every time we would have a cup of coffee at a café, we had to pass a security guard with a metal detector, and it was the same at food stores and shopping centers. The tension between the Israelis and Palestinians was, of course, unbearable. Jerusalem felt like anything but a city of peace.

But one learns to live with this tension, and eventually we felt very much at home. We made many prayer walks in the city and around Mount Zion. We made wonderful new friends and started with our work. In our free time, we had fellowship with different types of people from different backgrounds—Jews, Muslims, and Christians. And we came into contact with Catholics, who are everywhere in Jerusalem. In particular, we became acquainted with the Brothers and Sisters of religious Orders. They showed up at prayer groups, at church services, and in the Messianic congregations. Every Saturday we went to a congregation of Messianic Jews, and on Sundays we often went to the

Anglican congregation at the same church, Christ Church inside the Jaffa Gate.

Our apartment was situated in such a way that we saw the old walls of Jerusalem from our kitchen window. It was a beautiful sight, especially at night when the walls were flooded with golden light. We could hear the bells of the different churches ring. There were Catholic, Orthodox, Syrian, Armenian, Anglican, and Lutheran churches. Every Christian group, both ancient and new, seemed to be represented in Jerusalem.

All of this could be experienced in a concentrated way at the Church of the Holy Sepulchre. Here, the space is divided up between the different churches, and the services are scheduled with precision, so that all can have their needs met. There were rumors about conflicts between the Christians there, and there surely were such occurrences, but I must say that this was somewhat exaggerated. Despite all, ecumenism seemed to function rather well, at least as far as we could judge. During the great feast days, it could get a little heated at times, when the multitude of believers from different cultures crowded together to come into the church.

After having lived a year in central Jerusalem, we moved. For the following two years, we lived in the little village of Ein Kerem, a suburb in the western outskirts of Jerusalem. There we were able to rent a very nice house for our study center and information office. We had Bible studies and gave lectures about Israel to groups of visitors—pastors, students, and pilgrims. We provided information about our annual Israel tours and our work to assist the Russian Jews. I also gave seminars for Messianic pastors from around the country. Some of them were Russian Jews, some Israeli. Ein Kerem is the village where John the Baptist was born and the place where Mary, who was carrying Jesus in her womb, met Elizabeth, who was expecting John. That is to say, it is a place for blessed and important meetings.

Friends of ours, the Messianic Pastors Benjamin and Reuven Berger, also lived in Ein Kerem. Eventually, they introduced us to some of their Catholic friends. We were sometimes invited to an ecumenical prayer group, where many of these friends were present. I remember that once I found the prayer time a little dry and formal. But everyone was free to pray aloud, and at the end of the meeting I did so. Afterward, an elderly Franciscan dressed in his habit came up to me and asked who I was. I explained briefly that I was a Protestant pastor from Sweden. Then he looked at me and said he felt my prayer was really a prayer in the Holy Spirit. I was happily surprised that he accepted and confirmed my free style of prayer. In my ignorance, I had not expected that from a monk. When I asked where he lived, it turned out that he was a hermit and lived in a cave at Gethsemane! He added kindly that I was welcome to come and visit him. I could hardly believe my ears! Many prejudices were blown away in a single moment. This was all so new and very exciting for me.

Once I explained to a nun that she must understand that for me this thing with nuns was totally new. "At home in Sweden, we only see people like you on post cards", I said. She looked at me with great surprise, and it was obvious that she was not aware of how secularized Protestant Sweden is.

We began to meet charismatic Catholics a little here and there, and that was healthy for us. In some Protestant charismatic circles in which we were involved, there was, and is, a widespread idea that Catholics are not real Christians. It is with shame and pain that I write this. I know how Catholics have been wounded by these prejudices. The Catholic charismatics whom Birgitta and I met often had a much deeper understanding of the workings of the Spirit and of the Body of Christ and a greater love and humility than many of the Protestant charismatics we knew. This was a humbling experience for us, and we thanked God for taking us to task for the pride in our own lives.

One of those Catholics whom I benefited from meeting was Father Peter Hocken, an English priest. I heard about him through Reuven Berger and read his book *The Glory and the Shame*. It put into words all the thoughts I had regarding old churches and new movements. The book, in short, is about what is good and what is bad in the old established churches and the new movements, respectively, and how both need each other. He describes not only what could ideally be their contribution to each other but also the place of Messianic Jews in relation to both the established churches and the new movements. The book really struck a chord with me and became an important source of inspiration at that time. We met Father Peter Hocken in Israel in the fall of 2003, and Birgitta and I were surprised by how well we understood each other. We were particularly surprised that his use of theological language felt familiar, not foreign.

On one occasion, Birgitta and I were out for a walk in the valley below our house, the Yemenite Valley. While we were out walking in the beautiful terrain, among big rocks and olive trees, we passed a very old olive tree. Its stem was hollow, and the whole tree looked rotten. I casually thought that it was dead. But then I heard a clear question within me: "The tree looks dead, does it not?" I spontaneously thought, "Yes", without actually looking very carefully. "Look again!" came the words within me. I did so, and, to my surprise, I saw that the old tree was full of beautiful, small, fresh, green leaves. The tree was alive.

I then heard an admonition within me: "Never again say that something is dead." I realized that the Lord was rightly reproving me and that he was speaking to me of the historical churches. I had often judged from the surface and had been ignorant, proud, and arrogant. Then and there, I asked God's forgiveness for my prejudices and my bad attitude. I was ashamed, and from then on, I stopped calling other Christian denominations "dead". What did I know about the faith of other people? Nothing.

This entailed a healthy change in my thinking. I understood that it was impossible to come closer to the old churches without humility and gratitude. But if humility was there, a door slowly opened that would otherwise remain closed. I began to appreciate the Church more and more. I realized that I, just like the apostle Paul, had in fact lashed out at Christ by attacking other Christians. This was what Jesus said to Saul when he was thrown off his saddle on the way to Damascus in order to imprison Christians: "Saul, Saul, why do you persecute *me*?" (emphasis mine) (Acts 9:4).

I had not fully understood the intimate closeness that exists between Jesus and his Church, between the head and the limbs. I knew about it theoretically, of course, but now I began to realize how filled the Church actually is with the presence of Jesus and how close he always is to each and every one of us. Not only individually, by the fact that he lives in us, but also collectively, together with the other members. I understood that the Church was not only something problematic or a stepping-stone between Jesus and us. Jesus himself comes to us in and through his Church. Now I began to see in a new way how important the Church is. She is not only the receiver of God's grace but also the bearer of this grace. I began to love and discover the Church.

I realized how illusory it is to set the Church against the Scriptures or against the Gospel. It was wrong to choose between the faith of the Church and my personal faith. They must go together. The Church is necessary for my salvation, not an obstacle to it. She is the solution for and not the problem in my Christian life. That means that traditions, the liturgy, the ministries, dogmas, and other things, which many free churches think are heavy and uninteresting—yes, even a hindrance to the freedom of the Christian life—are instead what sustains the Christian life. The Spirit needs vessels. Life flows through the body. The Spirit's life is not a fleeting feeling but the life that continually keeps the body alive. The Spirit, who I knew is bound to the Scriptures, is also bound to the Body, the Church. It is the same with the human body. We cannot separate the body and the spirit without dying. It is also the same with the Body of Christ. If we separate the Spirit and the Body from each other, that separation will result in stagnation and death. The danger does not lie in the form but in formlessness.

Now an ecclesiological journey of discovery began that was completely revolutionary for me and that challenged most of what I had previously believed concerning the Body of Christ. The days of change now lay ahead of us.

Chapter 3

Birgitta: Looking Back and Looking Ahead

I came to Sweden as a ten-year-old, a little shy and a little timid. I had lived the greater part of my childhood in India as a child of missionaries. It had given me a rich and wonderful foundation in life, and I am so grateful for my childhood in the Indian countryside, in the state of Bihar in northern India. As small children, free from cares, we played with our Indian friends in the village, but when we reached school age, my siblings and I experienced the pain of being separated from our parents every school semester. The Swedish boarding school was located far away, down in southern India, a two-days' journey by train, and we were sent there. We would only see our parents for Christmas and summer holidays. Now, as an adult, I can see that we learned something about endurance during trials, but it was not easy.

When I was around thirteen, my father was assigned to Uppsala, Sweden, by the Methodist Church. I liked the city immediately, and I made good friends in my class at school. One of them was a daughter of the Lutheran priest[1] Fredrik

---

[1] The term "priest" is commonly used in the Lutheran Church in Sweden.

Sidwall, and over time, this servant of the Lord would come to mean a lot to me.

My parents had an ecumenical spirit. The borders between denominations did not seem to be important in our family. Naturally, in our Swedish context, this ecumenism was mainly a question of openness between free churches and the Swedish Lutheran Church. I did not hear much, either positive or negative, about the Catholic Church. I was confirmed in the Methodist Church, but later I became active in the Lutheran Church's youth group, where some of my classmates got involved after their confirmation. There I learned the Nicene Creed, which we read together every Friday evening after the youth group gathering. How I loved it! Such beautiful language! What depth that was transmitted to my teenage heart. We began to go to the Thursday communion services at Michael's church in Uppsala. During Pastor Fredrik Sidwall's years in this parish, a wonderful "revival of communion" was blooming among teenagers and university students. The church was so full that we often had to sit on the floor. The communion liturgy and Pastor Fredrik's short sermons were indelibly engraved in my heart.

But the human heart is often restless and unfaithful. After a few years, I lost contact with that spiritual lifeline. In my late teens, I treated my faith carelessly and pushed it to the side in favor of the usual pleasures of youth. I did not want to deny my Christian faith, but I was not a good witness. I was walking a thin line and had to be taught by costly experiences.

It was not until I was twenty-three years old that I surrendered and confessed my sin and asked the Lord to have mercy on me. A friend invited me to a charismatic meeting at Saint Peter's Methodist Church in Stockholm, and I remember that we were singing a beautiful hymn that I really loved. But I was afraid and was crying. My young life was in tatters, and only God could mend me. Some words in the hymn spoke to me about placing my soul in my Savior's hands. My heart was aching. For the first time in my life, I asked a pastor to pray with me and for me, and just at that moment, God gave me the grace of conversion. I did not understand it fully at the time, but that evening in Saint Peter's was a very important turning point for me. Relieved, I returned home with a heart filled with thankfulness and joy.

That was the fall of 1971, and the charismatic movement became my new spiritual homeland. This land consisted only of islands, however, without any structure or guidance. We were a group of friends who eagerly studied the Bible and prayed for each other. It was a wonderful time, and we wanted to grow in faith and follow Jesus. Nothing was more important than that. We could delve deeply into the Scriptures half the night and seek answers to our questions. Down the road I have lamented that we did not have any spiritual guides during those years, only ourselves. There is a great disadvantage in wanting to be so independent, and I believe it encouraged a certain spiritual pride in us.

~

A few years passed, and one day in May 1976, my youngest brother called me and gave me a tip about a Bible study out at Breidagård, a diocesan center just outside of Uppsala. We went there, and I found it a little difficult to concentrate during that Bible study. Right across from me, in the large circle of participants, I saw a young man whom I did not know. I noticed that our eyes met again and again. The

Bible study was followed by a coffee break, where we got a chance to talk a little bit. I was very excited to meet this very nice and good-looking man, and we decided to take a long walk together along the lake. During this walk, I began to get to know Ulf, a cheerful theologian and Navigator, and my heart beat with joy and delight. It is fun to remember that during this first walk we talked about the importance and beauty of the liturgy, of all subjects! Both of us had recently read the same books, and we were strongly attracted to what was called high-church spirituality. Despite the fact that I was so strongly influenced by the charismatic movement, and Ulf by the Navigators, a student movement with roots in the Calvinist tradition, we were united in our appreciation for the liturgy. We both desired a combination of rich liturgy and warm personal faith and revival. I went home from Breidagård and wondered if I would ever see him again.

We got married before Christmas that same year. What a joy and what a great blessing!

During the first years of our marriage, Ulf continued to study for his bachelor's degree in theology, and I worked as a secretary for an association for Christian students. We went to our local Lutheran church and sometimes also visited Saint Ansgar's high-church student congregation. We also had a prayer group once a week in our home. So, combining liturgical services and charismatic prayer in our lives was easy during that time. We were happy, and our family was growing. Ulf was ordained a priest and received his first ministry as a student chaplain in Uppsala, where he worked for a couple of years. Over time, a desire began to grow in us to be missionaries. Ulf felt that he wanted to take a sabbatical year to study the Bible in a deeper way, and at this time we heard about a Bible school in the United States called Rhema Bible Training Center.

~

A new period began for us with the school year of 1981–
1982 in the United States. For a young Swedish family with
children, it was naturally very exciting to live in Oklahoma
for a year. Back in Sweden, kids were not allowed to sit
freely out in the back of a pick-up truck in traffic. Nor did
one often see a rifle hanging in the back window of said
pickup truck. We saw things that amazed us. We also came
across many new things in the churches, for example, a perfect Sunday school system and a nursery for the small children. After some time of adjustment, I was able to leave our
boys in their groups, and I could finally participate in the
service undisturbed. In our Lutheran churches back home,
there was at this point in time no Sunday school during services or any chance to leave your smallest kids to be cared
for in a playroom. Here we found this luxury, and, having
three little boys, I was so grateful.

Theologically, there was of course much that affected us.
What we liked was the great emphasis on living in and from
God's Word. We loved the songs of praise and the fresh faith
and expectation that God moves concretely in people's lives.
We were a group of about six Swedish students who willingly absorbed the American attitude that everything is possible. But their idea of just starting a new church on one's
own was very foreign to us. When we went to the United
States, our sights were focused on missionary life somewhere, wherever the Lord wanted to send us. But in the
spring semester, we realized that we should go back to Sweden where Ulf wanted very much to start a Christian Bible
school for all denominations. We really wanted to work to
strengthen young Christians in their faith and to teach them
to know God's Word and the Holy Spirit. At this point in
time, our love for the church's liturgy and structured forms

was totally pushed out of sight by all the new things that we experienced.

When we came back to Sweden, Ulf had no job to return to, and we had to adjust to a new reality. Even in the United States, we had struggled financially. But Ulf became known rather quickly as an interesting, zealous young Lutheran priest through a few articles in free-church newspapers and a series of meetings in an independent Pentecostal church in Stockholm. It was a year when Ulf traveled all around the country as an itinerant preacher, while at the same time we planned for our Bible school, which we intended to start in the fall of 1983. We named it Word of Life. Ulf also had public Bible studies in Uppsala, and eventually our resistance to "starting a new church" broke down, and we decided we needed to do that, also.

～

God sees the intentions and desires of our hearts, and he has been so good to us. We wanted to serve him with all our hearts and did so for thirty years in Word of Life church. These were spiritually rich years. They were also years when we experienced opposition and suffering of different kinds. Despite the difficulties, thousands of young Christians were able to deepen their faith by studying in our Bible school. Many learned to share their faith both in Sweden and in different mission fields, and during the 1990s, Word of Life experienced a mission epoch that was fantastic.

For those unfamiliar, Word of Life is a nondenominational church, and when we founded it, it was one of the first in our nation. We knew that this would disturb the peace and quiet in Sweden, but we could not have imagined how much. We were heavily criticized in the media, both Christian and secular. You just do not start new churches in

Sweden! But in spite of the criticism, hundreds and eventually thousands came to our Bible school. Both young and old loved the faith-filled preaching and teaching. From the humble beginning with only around twenty university students, our church grew steadily to one thousand, two thousand, and finally around three thousand members. It was actually quite amazing to experience this growth. In Sweden, it was simply astounding. Each summer and New Year we organized big conferences with thousands in attendance. People from many nations started to come to see what was happening in Uppsala. Our teaching was focused on faith, the Lord's power to heal and restore, the need to evangelize and preach the Gospel to every nation, and prayer. People were very encouraged in their faith, and so were we. After a few years, we outgrew our first rented facility and took a bold step of faith when we built a new facility with a church hall that could seat four thousand people. This was front-page news in the national newspapers. We were very happy and proud. The people who came to Word of Life came from every direction—Pentecostals and other free-church people as well as Lutherans. Many non-believers came to faith, and we also saw many Muslims come to faith in Jesus Christ and be baptized.

From the start, we had to struggle with the Swedish school authorities and government because we definitely wanted to start a Christian school for the children in our congregation. This was not at all appreciated by our Social Democratic government. But we knew our rights and stood our ground. The school was started, and after some years we had our miracle when the school finally was subsidized by the State. Now many hundreds of children have gone through this school, and it is still an excellent school with hundreds of students attending through high school.

During the eighties and half of the nineties, we did not

spend any time thinking of the historic churches as we were totally focused on our work with Word of Life in Sweden and abroad.

~

Every summer we took hundreds of pilgrims on a trip through the Holy Land, and our children came along. Over time, Israel became like a second homeland to us. To get to know Israel, the land where Jesus was born, worked, suffered, died, and rose was an invaluable experience for us. We wanted to learn everything and see everything in this very special country. Privately, we drove around with the boys, stopped at different places and recounted what had happened there in the history of the Bible. We saw it as a great grace to be so at home in the Lord's own land.

Through our close contact with Russia, our eyes were opened to the difficult situation of the Russian Jews in a country that had suffered from anti-Semitism for centuries. Many suffered terribly from persecution. Therefore, we started a humanitarian organization that led many thousands of Jews to Israel. For some years, Word of Life owned a ship that was equipped to transport Russian Jews from Russia to Israel. In November 1995, Ulf and I boarded the ship when it passed Istanbul. On this journey from Russia to Haifa, there were fifty-eight Jews, and it was a moving experience to see them standing by the railing on the lookout for their ancient homeland. Song and dance broke out when Haifa's light became visible on the horizon. The prophecy of Isaiah was fulfilled before our eyes:

> Fear not, for I am with you;
> I will bring your offspring from the east,
> and from the west I will gather you;

I will say to the north, Give up,
   and to the south, Do not withhold;
bring my sons from afar
   and my daughters from the end of the earth.
(Is 43:5–6)

~

Right at this time, the fall of 1995, there was also something else that began to grow in me and demand my attention. Our congregation had existed for twelve years, and I
began to miss certain things that I used to love. The feeling
was diffuse, but there was one thing I knew; I wanted to
see Pastor Fredrik Sidwall one more time and experience a
communion service with him. I did not even know if he was
still alive. That fall, I often looked in our local newspaper to
see if his name would appear in the church announcements.
Suddenly it happened! I saw that he would be celebrating
the mass at Holy Trinity Lutheran church the first Sunday
of Advent at 8 o'clock in the morning! I was overjoyed! Our
family would, of course, go to the service at Word of Life,
but I promised that I would be back in time.

It is difficult to describe the joy and sense of anticipation
I felt when I sat down in the church pew in this beautiful
old church from the fourteenth century. There were only
a few early birds there. My heart warmed with love and
gratitude when I saw Pastor Fredrik, the dear priest of my
youth, come in. The liturgy of the mass, the prayers, and
the words of the ritual itself were still so familiar to me. It
was as though no time had passed since the 1970s. I was
lifted up into the Lord's presence. Toward the end of the
service, I stood in the center aisle and wondered doubtfully
if Pastor Fredrik had recognized me, despite the fact that so

many years had passed since we had seen each other. Then he came toward me with outstretched arms, and a broad smile spread across his face. He hugged me and said: "We know, of course, that the Lord comes into his Church on the First Sunday of Advent, but this year Birgitta came also!" We laughed heartily and spoke a little. What a wonderful reunion! I practically flew home. This joy was more than joy over the reunion with a beloved priest. It was also a deep joy over holy communion, over the priestly ministry, and over my fumbling effort to reconnect with the old church.

~

Ulf truly rejoiced with me. This experience became a seed planted down deep in the seed ground of my heart. We lived a demanding life with many obligations. We were so busy with the work of our church, our intensive missionary work in Russia and other nations, and with all our trips to Israel. Now we even began to do pastors' conferences in India, and it was fantastic for me to reconnect with the land of my childhood.

One day we saw a report on television about Taizé in France. We saw how young people flocked there by the thousands in order to worship the Lord with beautiful songs and in reverent silence. How was it possible that so many young people loved this? There was no happy teenage preaching here, no modern songs of praise. Nevertheless, the stream never ended, and year after year, thousands of young people came to this little village in France. We decided that we would go there and see. So, in June 1999, we flew there with Joakim and Maria Lundqvist. Joakim was then the youth pastor at Word of Life. We really loved the worship in Taizé and met and talked to some of the Brothers there. What impressed us most profoundly was to meet and sit and talk to Brother Roger, the founder of the community. While we talked, he held Ulf's hand and did not let go of it until he was finished talking to us. We treasure this memory, particularly since Brother Roger was murdered in 2005.

While we were in this area of France, we also took the opportunity to see Cluny. Ulf, who is very good at history, told us about its era of greatness. The monastery there had been founded in the tenth century, and the church that was built there was Christianity's largest for many centuries. During the French Revolution, the beautiful church had been demolished to its foundation. But the Church cannot be destroyed; God himself dwells within her. We walked around the ruins and sang songs of praise to God.

In August of the same summer, we ventured out to the annual meeting of the high-church Lutherans in Uppsala. This group was comprised of more conservative members within the Swedish church. We had friends there whom we had known since our days as students, and it was nice to meet some of them again. Ulf was especially glad to renew contact with Bishop Bertil Gärtner, who had ordained him a priest.

Obviously, something had begun to happen in us that we did not exactly know how to interpret. It was an extremely personal journey, a longing for depth, and an anchoring in something that was greater than our own denomination. We felt no need to express this process publicly, as we were hardly conscious of it ourselves.

As Ulf told in a previous chapter, in October 1999, we traveled together to Rome for the first time. I had been there as a ten-year-old on the way home from India, and Ulf had been there in the spring of 1976, just before we met.

As all travelers to Rome do, we walked around and enjoyed all the beauty. We were happy about all the fantastic churches, but we did not understand all those statues and pictures of the Virgin Mary. As a Protestant, one is worried that anyone should take the place of Jesus, and in this regard we were concerned.

We had found a hotel room just a stone's throw away from Saint Peter's Basilica, and on two occasions, we saw and heard Pope John Paul II. At the Angelus prayer, where the pope preaches from his window, he spoke on a subject that definitely captured our attention. He told that just that day, October 31, 1999, Lutherans and Catholics had signed a common declaration regarding justification by faith. Here we were, standing in Saint Peter's Square, in the center of Rome, and we heard that Catholics and Lutherans had now made an end to the conflict that began with Martin Luther and caused the great division in Christendom. So remarkable! So historical! The reason for the "protest" was no longer there.

~

When the new millennium began, a new period began for us, also. We moved from our house with our youngest son to a flat in the center of Uppsala. Our nearest neighbor then became the Catholic parish of Saint Lars, which is located very nicely by the river in the center of Uppsala. From our kitchen window, we had a glorious view of Uppsala's cathedral. Ulf has always been interested in Church history, so now he was happy to take the opportunity to improve his knowledge of it. He contacted the professor of Church history, and so it happened that he participated for a couple of semesters in a research seminar and spent many hours at Carolina Rediviva, the fine library at the University of Uppsala.

At that time, we had no desire to visit Saint Lars Catholic Church for Mass, but we did go there for their Christmas market, and on a few occasions Ulf helped a nun break up the ice on the sidewalk. We used to go swimming at the central swimming hall at that time, and sometimes we walked back home together with another of the nuns, who also liked to use the swimming facility. We appreciated talking to this nice Sister.

For some years now, Word of Life had also had a small university in cooperation with Oral Roberts University in Tulsa, and I myself took a course in early Church history at Word of Life University. I found Church history very interesting. Naturally, I was taken by those personalities from the first centuries. The witness of the martyrs and the Apostolic Fathers put everything in the right perspective. Not only Ulf and I but many in our church took the opportunity to dig deeper and learn more about early Christian history and theology. It was a good time, and our congregation enjoyed Ulf's sermons on unity in the Body of Christ.

In October 2001, my dear youth ministry priest Fredrik Sidwall died. We went to his funeral in the cathedral. The church was full of priests! It was obvious that Sidwall had meant a great deal to many. My heart was filled with gratitude when I sat there and saw his simple pine casket. We followed the crowd a little hesitantly out to the reception afterward. He had himself decided that at the funeral reception, not only would coffee and cake be served but also a warm soup! That wonderful shepherd!

Ulf and I had become accustomed to being met with suspicion and direct hostility. The judgments made against Word of Life were hard for many years. We were therefore so astonished when many high-church priests hugged Ulf and said encouraging words. Suddenly, Ulf was nearly lifted off the ground when strong arms hugged him from behind in the crowd. It was a Brother from Östanbäck's Lutheran

Benedictine monastery. We had not seen him since Ulf was a student chaplain and this Brother was a young theology student. When he burst out with the words: "I have prayed for both of you every day since then!" we were extremely touched and full of wonder.

This encounter resulted in our contacting Father Caesarius at Östanbäck, and later that winter we went there for the first time. For Ulf, it was a dear reunion to meet his old professor. I had never met Father Caesarius myself but had heard Ulf often speak so respectfully about this man, who had been his favorite teacher during his study years.

When I look back now, I see how God, even early on, allowed many small signs and road markers to lead us forward. The walls between the historical Church and us began slowly to crack in our minds. But we could still not stretch ourselves as far as the Catholic Church; rather, it was mostly reconciliation with the Swedish Lutheran church that remained in our thoughts.

~

During the year 2001, Ulf and I began to talk with each other about being missionaries ourselves. We wanted to be flexible and to obey the Lord. Our youngest son was now an adult, and the Word of Life congregation was stable and could give its consent for us to move out to the mission field. We intended to go to India, but as Ulf has written, God had other plans.

It was now 2002, and during our long tour in Asia that spring, I read a thick novel about Saint Birgitta. Before the seven hundredth Jubilee year of her birth (1303), there was a newly awakened interest in her, and since my name is Birgitta, I felt that it was time for me to become a little better acquainted with this Swedish saint.

I was completely fascinated by Birgitta Birgersdotter! I got hold of all the available books about her and enjoyed getting to know fourteenth-century Sweden. Birgitta herself was such a radiant Christian that one could not help being captivated by her. Already as a child, she had received some strong spiritual experiences, which are moving to read about. When Birgitta was only seven years old, she had a vision of a beautiful Lady who offered her a golden crown, which she accepted. She could feel it touch her forehead. As a ten-year-old girl she contemplated the pain Christ was suffering on the Cross, and she asked him who had done this to him. Jesus answered her: "Those who have contempt for me and despise my love".

One thing that impressed me was how careful she was as an adult not to be spiritually led astray. Birgitta had many revelations of Jesus and Mary. But she always hurried to her confessor in order to be assured that what she had heard or seen in her revelations was not a "delusion" from the devil. She would rather die than assert something that was not in accord with Scripture and Christian doctrine, however powerful the revelation might have been. I thought of how people today gladly and very often flippantly claim that God has revealed this or that to them without being terribly interested in self-critique. That gave me respect for her.

When we came home to Sweden in the summer, I spent much time reading many books about Saint Birgitta, and over time we visited Finsta, Vadstena, and also Ulvåsa, where she lived. It was so special to walk around the ruins of the home where she and her husband lived at the cape of Lake Boren. She gave birth to eight children there and ran the large household, took in the poor, the sick, and even "fallen women". Of course, it did not escape us that the couple had the same names as Ulf and I did! When her husband, Ulf, died, she went to live in Rome and eventually founded the Brigittine Order.

Naturally, there was one thing that was difficult for me to swallow as a Protestant—her relationship to the Virgin Mary. How could I understand that? I did not at all question the fact that Birgitta's supernatural experiences were inspired. As Christians, we know that God speaks to us through the Holy Spirit, and we know that he can work signs and wonders. But Mary? It was so difficult for me to believe or accept that one could speak with Mary or that Mary would have so active a role as she had in Birgitta's life. I did see the Virgin Mary as a blessed and venerable person, but she had died and was now in heaven. This is how we thought. And as a Protestant, I would gladly quote the Old Testament's prohibition about seeking contact with the dead. This was all a little troublesome. I could not put it all together, especially since I knew how careful Birgitta was with theology and right doctrine. Saint Birgitta forced me to go deeper.

∼

On August 7, 2002, we moved into a little apartment in Yemin Moshe outside Jerusalem's old city wall. That was a wonderful adventure for us. We knew the country well, since we had led pilgrim tours there for fifteen years. But to be able to live there was different. It felt like a grace. When I stood washing dishes, I heard the church bells ringing in the old city, and when the sun went down, the wall was golden colored. Through the years, we had often admired this beautiful and unique district where artists lived, and now we lived here. And outside our window, there stood a fig tree, which spread its mysterious and sweet fragrance.

A few days after we arrived in Jerusalem, we took a quiet walk in the Christian quarters in the Old City of Jerusalem. We walked on a small lane without peddlers or crowds. Then I saw something that caught my attention. In a shop window, there were beautifully painted ceramic bowls and one lone little unpainted figurine, made of white clay. It was Mary with her little boy, Jesus, who was standing beside her, half hidden by his mother's dress. In her other hand, she held a water jug. This ceramic figurine differed greatly from so many other things that, to a Swede, can appear like kitsch at a market in the Middle East. We went in and looked at the articles, and I could not resist buying the Marian figurine. The items were signed with the word "Bethlehem" and a little star. The shop owner said that nuns had made them. Where this simple and beautiful figurine would lead us, we could not have imagined at the time.

We needed to find a church with an English-speaking service and tried Christ Church inside the Jaffa Gate, which was in walking distance from our home. This is an Anglican church, and it felt nice for us, since it was easy to recognize the liturgy, which reminds one of the liturgy of the Swedish church. There was a priest there by the name of Cohen, an Englishman with a Jewish background. We very much appreciated both the Anglican and the Jewish elements that were present in the service. Among other hymns, we sang the *Sh'ma Israel*, the ancient Jewish confession: "Hear O Israel, the Lord our God, the Lord is One." Unfortunately, Cohen finished working as priest in that parish just half a year later, but over time, we had come to know the Messianic pastors Benjamin and Reuven Berger, who had services in the same church on the Sabbath. It was natural for us to begin going there instead, and we remained there during our three years in Jerusalem. Their services were in Hebrew, but the sermons were interpreted for us foreigners with headphones. We learned many hymns in Hebrew, but I often missed the Anglican services and the wonderful English hymns.

The division within Christianity becomes so evident in a city like Jerusalem. I do not mean that there is fighting between the churches, only that one sees so many trends and specific forms that differ from each other. Greek Catholic, Greek Orthodox, Roman Catholic, Maronite, Arameans, Copts, Armenians, Assyrians, Anglicans, Protestant, Hebrew Catholic and Messianic Jews—all mingle in this old and amazing city. We came to realize that we were also a part of the division in the Body of Christ. It became important for us to pray for Christian unity. I remember how, during our first year there, we had a visit from other Word of Life pastors, and we stood on a balcony looking out over the city and all its churches and prayed for God's blessing over them, that he would unite his divided Body.

~

In March 2003, the war in Iraq broke out. Everyone in Israel had to obtain a gas mask, and we dutifully got ours. One was supposed to have it strapped over one's shoulder at all times. It seemed a little surrealistic, but we realized that the threat was real. There was talk about the danger of bombs with poisonous gas. To live among relatives to the Jews who were gassed by Hitler during World War II and now had to fear that they themselves could share the same destiny was indeed painful. We suffered alongside the Jewish people.

During the years we lived in Israel, we experienced the terror close up. This is what I wrote in my pocket calendar during 2003 alone: "March 5—Bus bomb in Haifa, fifteen dead; June 11—Bus bomb on Jaffa Street, seventeen

dead, sixty wounded; September 9—Bomb at bus station
in Tel Aviv, seven dead; and on the same day a bomb at
Café Hillel, where we usually went for coffee—five dead,
one of them a young girl who was to be married the next
day; October 3—Woman suicide bomber at a restaurant in
Haifa, nineteen dead and thirteen wounded." We saw under
these conditions something that moved us deeply. In peace
times, all the different Jewish groups and political parties
can quibble as much as they like; they live in a democracy.
But in times of external threat, they become one family in
a single second, *Bet Israel*, the House of Israel. After an act
of terrorism toward Israeli civilians, the *Jerusalem Post* was
filled with photos of the dead and moving obituaries about
them, each one of them. The Israelis grieved over the dead
as if they were family members.

~

We came home to Sweden again in May 2003 on our summer vacation, and it was good to share our learning and experiences with our home congregation. The year in Jerusalem
had changed us in a positive way. Ulf often spoke now
about going deeper and broadening, and our congregation
was open and responsive to this. Now we began to publish
Word of Life's new theological magazine *Keryx*. Our son
Benjamin had taken the initiative to start it and was its editor. Writing articles for *Keryx* forced Ulf to concentrate on
certain theological subjects, and he was quite content with
that. We realized that in our free-church context, there was
a need for a magazine with theological substance.

Chapter 4

Ulf: Jerusalem—
Introduction to Something New

It was wonderful to live in Israel. We learned so much, had many wonderful experiences, and made many new friends. But we were not there the entire time during those years. Jerusalem served as our home base, but our responsibility for Word of Life's international work involved a great deal of traveling over the whole world. There were many trips: to Russia, Armenia, and the Ukraine, but also to the Far East, Singapore, Taiwan, and a few other countries. During our first year in Israel, we had some quieter periods, and I had the opportunity of writing a book about spiritual leadership.

In Jerusalem, we had gotten to know a group of ecumenically minded young Catholics, Koinonia Giovanni Battista, through the Berger brothers. In November 2003, they invited us to visit them in Italy. Birgitta and I were going to Milan for a Protestant charismatic conference. After that conference, we met up with some of our friends in the Koinonia community and traveled with them to one of their centers in Northern Italy. The center was located in a beautiful mountain district, and it was so rewarding to meet with them and see their beautiful fellowship, love, and unity. We also went with them to Rome, where they showed us around the city and guided us through Saint Peter's Basilica. We knelt there together and prayed for the unity of the Church before the high altar in the nave of the church. The conviction about the great need for visible unity among Christians penetrated our hearts ever more deeply.

Koinonia was a charismatic and evangelizing Catholic community. They had also been exposed to some Protestant charismatic faith instruction. It was an eye-opener for us to see that there were young Catholics who were in many respects so much like us. Through this meeting, a lot of our prejudices fell away. The fellowship with them was refreshing and was our first real contact with a larger group of young Catholics.

At home in Jerusalem, we used to make use of our free time by walking around in the old city and visiting the churches there. It was fascinating to go into them, not least of all the Oriental churches. Step by step, our ignorance and prejudices surrounding these historical churches disappeared, and a feeling of recognition presented itself. I began to see them as bearers of spiritual treasures. I was often inside the Church of the Holy Sepulchre, and I loved to sit by the Golgotha Rock and pray there. It was almost unreal to realize that one was actually only a few yards away from the place where, according to tradition, Jesus was crucified. It was here that he died for my sins and the sins of all mankind. Sometimes it was quiet and peaceful at this very important place, but often it was filled with pilgrims and was rather busy, as was typical of the Middle East. This busyness was surely rather like the environment in Jesus' own time.

Sometimes we made prayer walks around Mount Zion and often visited the Dormition Abbey, which is located up on Mount Zion. It is enchantingly beautiful, with its large mosaic of Jesus and his Mother that adorns the apse and dominates the whole church. The crypt under the church is one, single, artistic, and beautiful homage to Mary and her dormition. In this church, we felt we could be a little more in peace. We often went there to pray.

An advantage of living in Jerusalem was that we had a little more free time to read and study. At home in Sweden, our hectic life had limited our reading to only what was most necessary. It felt so satisfying to have more time for reading. To have Catholic books on your bookshelf was a bit risky, and some of our friends looked somewhat surprised when they saw these book titles in our home. At the same time, we knew that it was completely necessary to begin exploring Catholic theology and spirituality more seriously. After all, it was the largest Christian church, and I needed to consult its sources to know what its members believed.

During a preaching tour in the United States in May 2004, I was in Seattle. I went into an ordinary bookstore and looked around a little among the books in the religion section. I was there with some Protestant friends and was not courageous enough to speak about my growing interest in the Catholic faith. On the bookshelf, there was a book that almost jumped out at me. That is how I experienced it. The book was brown, with a photo on the front cover of a nun. I had never heard of her. I looked at it a little distract-edly, wondered if I should buy it, but then put it back and continued on. I went another time around the shop, and, without thinking about it, I came back and saw that book again. It almost signaled to me. I looked at it a little more but put it back. I had taken a few other books, and it was time to go. I stood in line with our friends and paid. But when we had gone through the checkout, I said to them that I had forgotten a book, asked them to wait, and went quickly back, bought the book, and put it hurriedly into my bag. The book was called *The Life of Faustina Kowalska*, by Sister Sophia Michalenko. I was a little nervous about the book and did not show it to them. I had no desire to start a discussion then and there.

As I read it, a whole new and unknown world opened up for me. Faustina's life was incredibly fascinating. Naturally, her cloistered life was something completely foreign, but in the description of her journey, there was much that I recognized, not the least when it had to do with the life of prayer. There were many points that touched me, in particular the subject of intercessory prayer and the carrying of others in a prayerful struggle for the good of their souls.

What was new and challenging for me, and where I also began to find explanations, was the view of suffering. It differed in many ways from what I was used to in Word of Life. During the past years, I had begun to study and teach more about suffering, its place and function. Now I was being taught by a Sister who had experienced much suffering and who could give me good explanations. Completely new to me was the idea of uniting one's sufferings with Christ on the Cross, offering up difficulties, and in that way allowing the suffering to be transformed into something that builds up the Body of Christ. Then, when I saw the biblical references, I was astonished. I had often pondered over what the apostle Paul actually meant when he said in Colossians 1:24: "Now I rejoice in my sufferings for your sake, and in my flesh I complete what is lacking in Christ's afflictions for the sake of his body, that is, the Church." Now I was beginning to see a dimension of suffering and its function that I had never known anything about before. Faustina's life became, in a way, a road sign for me, and I read the book again and again.

In my spiritual context, we taught that the suffering that we Christians were to endure mainly came from the outside, such as opposition and persecution against the faith. In the light of the healing ministry of Jesus—where Jesus in the Gospel always healed all the sick that came to him—I had a hard time understanding that suffering through sickness was something to embrace. I surely saw sickness more as an enemy than a blessing. I had to reflect over the positive side of suffering and started to understand the benefits of the way in which we can give our sufferings to the Lord— and what he can do through these acts of uniting ourselves to the Cross. The whole concept of carrying the suffering of others in a co-redemptive way was altogether new to me.

~

I had now gradually begun to realize how little I knew about Pope John Paul II, despite the fact that he had been pope for more than twenty-five years. In 1989, I had publicly criticized his visit to Sweden in some negative articles I had written, but I knew nothing about his life and ministry. This made me feel ashamed, and I realized that I must do something about it. I got some books about him and devoured George Weigel's great biography, *Witness to Hope*. It was incredibly fascinating to read about his life. I realized more and more what a spiritual giant this man was. I also realized what a huge gap there had been between my smaller spiritual world and the great spiritual world in which John Paul II lived and worked. To see into his world was overwhelming. It was very interesting to learn about his upbringing, his spiritual development, his sufferings, his prayer life, and his self-giving attitude toward life. I realized how much I had missed out on when I chose to ignore him! It was something that made me very sad and for which I had to make amends to God. Later, on one occasion, when I was visiting at home in Sweden, a journalist asked me if there was anything in my life that I regretted. It was almost a little comical to see the surprise on his face when I said that if there was anything I regretted, it was that for so many years I had completely missed out on the life, ministry, and great meaning of John Paul II for the world.

It was nevertheless so enriching to watch him and study him in the remaining years of his life. His resistance to Nazism and Communism, his courage, and his total surrender to God were so impressive; his powerful actions that led so concretely to the fall of the Iron Curtain.

There is no doubt that Pope John Paul II was the man who, together with Ronald Reagan and President Mikhail Gorbachev, was most responsible for the collapse of the Soviet Union. I was astonished when I saw films of the pope's visit to Poland in 1979 and how the entire people defied the Communists and let themselves be renewed in faith by the pope's speech. He was a fiery preacher and evangelist. Poland's future destiny was decided there—and I had missed out on knowing about this man! But as Birgitta and I learned about what really happened through John Paul II's history and what had brought about these historical changes, we were deeply moved.

I felt a great admiration for him in this because it had made it possible for us to throw ourselves into a great missionary work in the East as soon as the Iron Curtain fell. I remember how Birgitta and I, along with some friends, felt called to travel to Moscow the day after Christmas in 1991. It proved to be a historical day, and we found ourselves standing in Red Square seeing Russia's new flag blowing in the wind for the first time since the red banner of the Soviet Union had been lowered.

In Russia, and in the former Soviet Union, with its satellite states, we were able to be a part of great and remarkable
things when we preached the Gospel everywhere.

Now I started again to study him more carefully. It was
so moving to watch him on television those last years when
he fought his illness, bore his sufferings in such an amazing
way, and continued to serve Jesus and the Church so un-
tiringly, right up to his last breath. We watched his funeral
from a hotel room in Singapore together with millions of
other television viewers around the world who were moved
whether they believed in God or not.

~

One evening in Jerusalem, in the fall of 2002, we had heard
something that puzzled us. A few of us sat and talked at a
café near the Jaffa Gate in the Old City. One person in the
group was an alumnus of Word of Life's Bible School in
Uppsala. He was a Croatian, with a Catholic background,
who had become a Protestant and had lived in Sweden for
some years. He began to tell about Marian apparitions in
a small town called Medjugorje in Bosnia-Herzegovina, on
the border of Croatia. He had been there himself and was
both skeptical and impressed. He had seen so many convert
to the Lord there, he said, and many had received vocations
to the priesthood there. I had never heard of this. It was
something totally new, and Birgitta and I naturally became
a little curious. How could this, which I believed was something wrong, result in so many young people becoming on
fire for Jesus? In my Protestant mind, this did not make
sense.

I had heard about Lourdes and Fatima in a superficial way,
but I had filtered this out, due to very negative sources of
information. For me, in my ignorance, they were examples

of how crazy things could become. It was completely against all Protestant theology even to come near so-called Marian apparitions. We read a little about Medjugorje and thought that we could perhaps look into what it was all about at some point. We heard that millions of people had visited this place since the 1980s.

I had routinely gotten the impression that Catholics worshipped Mary in the same way we Protestants prayed to God. That was not difficult to see, I thought. There were numerous photos of people who knelt before pictures, icons, and statues of Mary. And there were all kinds of complicated titles for her and an enormous number of prayer books. The classical Protestant diagnosis of all this, springing from the Bible's prohibition of images, was that this was some form of idol worship.

But now, I was beginning to understand more and more how important and central the Virgin Mary is for our common faith in Jesus Christ. I had not thought out fully before how intimately Mary was connected with Christology, that is, the view of the necessity that Jesus is both God and man. I knew how important it was to have a correct view of Jesus, which in turn gives a correct view of salvation. The Incarnation is central and necessary to our faith.

Jesus took his human nature from Mary. He was not divided into two independent parts, a human and a divine, but, rather, he was *one* human being, both divine and human, who grew inside the womb of Mary. This little child *is* God. He is the second Person of the Godhead, God the Son, who came to us "in the flesh", for the sake of our salvation. That is what the Incarnation means.

Without Mary's consent and cooperation, her Yes, Jesus could not become man, and, without Jesus, there is no salvation, either for us or for Mary. Without Jesus, Mary is nothing. Her importance comes completely from him, and she also constantly points to him. Mary is uniquely blessed in order to be the Mother of the Lord (Lk 1:43), since the Child she bore is God's own Son. That is why the Church has called her the Mother of God. Not the Mother of God the Father—he has no mother—but the Mother of God the Son, since he is God who became a human being through her. Mary is therefore completely unique. No other woman has ever had such a great mission. This has only happened once and will never happen in this way again. It is no wonder that all generations should call her blessed (Lk 1:48).

I myself had never called her blessed. The questions surrounding Mary troubled me, and I had instinctively let her remain in the background. Neither in my preaching nor in my life did she have any prominent place.

When Mary's place in God's plan of salvation became clearer to me and she appeared to be so important, I could understand that one would readily wish to honor her. In a more southern European way, she is venerated with beautiful titles of honor, statues, and feast days. I began to understand now that this had nothing to do with idol worship. I realized that one does not worship someone as God just because one bows or shows respect in different ways like Catholics do to Mary. We do the same when we show respect for certain people. It was, however, culturally different from the more reserved Scandinavian way of expression that I was used to.

The Church distinguishes carefully between worship—which is reserved only for the Triune God—and veneration, which is shown to Mary to honor her. Mary is not worshipped as God. However, one can ask for the intercessory prayers of Mary and the saints in the same way one can ask other Christians for their prayers. Mary and the saints live in heaven to worship God and to pray for and with us, that God's will shall be done, on earth as it is in heaven (Rev 4:10, 5:8). They are, in fact, more alive than we are, and we are united as members in the same Body of Christ—a Body that exists both in heaven and on earth. As a Protestant, I was not accustomed to thinking that heaven cooperated with earth in this way.[1]

When I looked through the Bible more carefully, I saw how much, in fact, there was about Mary. In a routine fashion, I had the idea that the Bible did not seem to say much about her. Consequently, I ignored everything that the Evangelists actually say about Mary. She was there at the Annunciation and the Birth of Jesus and when he was presented in the Temple. She walked with him in his ministry. She stood close to the Cross at his death. She was even there in the account in the Book of Acts about the birth of the Church in the Upper Room, with the outpouring of the Holy Spirit. In all of these important events, Mary was present.

∼

The discovery of Mary in the Bible even led to my thinking more about the use of the Bible and the place of the Bible in the life of the Church. From my first moment as a Christian, I had learned how important the Bible is as God's own Word to us. I had quickly accepted the evangelical theological formulation "Scripture alone".

The Church has read, believed, and revered the Bible as God's Word through all the ages. The claim that Christians did not have access to the Bible before the Reformation is, in fact, not true. Of course, everyone did not walk around

---

[1] See the *Catechism of the Catholic Church*, 2nd ed. (Vatican City: Libreria Editrice Vaticana, 1997; Washington, D.C.: United States Catholic Conference, 2000), no. 971.

with his own Bible under his arm as we can do today, but it had more to do with the time of Gutenberg's invention of the printing press. In the early Church and during the Middle Ages, there were no printing presses, and the ordinary parish member did not have his own New Testament at home. However, Scriptures were read during the liturgy. The congregation listened, prayed, and believed together. The liturgy proclaimed the Word, the homily explained the Word, and the congregation lived out and kept the Word. The homily as a phenomenon did not begin at the Reformation, but, rather, preaching had been important from the very beginning of the Church.

The idea of "Scripture alone", on the contrary, did not exist in the Church for the first fifteen hundred years. Nor is that thought expressed in the Bible itself. The fact that nowhere in the Bible does it say which books are actually canonical or how they came to be in the canon makes it completely natural to look outside the Bible itself in order to get a correct understanding both of the Bible and of Christian life.

For me, "Scripture alone" just meant that I believed in the Scriptures and wanted to be faithful to God's Word that is in the Bible. But I began to realize that one must make use of some form of experience or tradition that was not described in detail in the Bible. It was easy to see that not only the Catholic Church but, in fact, every denomination and movement has different traditions and experiences that have developed through the years and are believed to have their foundation explicitly or implicitly in the Bible. What distinguishes them however, is the difference between traditions in general and Tradition with a capital T.

In the Catholic Church, there is both an authoritative experience and understanding that have been passed down as well as a genuine apostolic teaching ministry that can and should interpret the Scriptures and can point out what the Church teaches and should believe when different problems arise. This visible authority, with legitimate interpreters, proved to be a great strength but also a stumbling block for outsiders.

As a Catholic, one does not consider oneself the final authority, which is so often the case in the Protestant milieu. To understand and to explain everything oneself creates many individual opinions and disparate ideas, which makes it difficult to assert what is actually right and what is wrong when confronted with opponents. It hardly helps to maintain that the Spirit is the interpreter, since wonderful people, who all seem to have the Spirit, come to different conclusions.

There is a great strength in the authority of the Catholic teaching office, a storehouse of experience from which to draw, and a sense of peace and rest in the fact that God has given the Church an authentic teaching office that, led by the Holy Spirit, can teach, lead, and explain what the apostolic faith is. This faith should be received personally so that it might truly be alive in the believer's own life. Then it becomes a personal, living faith for each one.

This was an important discovery for me: instead of us carrying the Church, the Church carries us and even believes through us. It was also a challenge to trust that Jesus is very present in the visible Church, which is his Body, and he can speak and act through her different members. The expression: "Trust in the Church" now became logical to me.

Tradition, with a capital T, is not a question of an abundance of different traditions and human ideas; rather, it means, as does the word *traditio*, to *transmit* correctly and *receive* God's revelation, so that it can be *passed down* authentically from generation to generation. Simply expressed, Tradition is the spiritual experience that the Church has transmitted. It is everything that the Church, led by the Spirit, has been led to receive, practice, and pass down. In the Second Letter to the Thessalonians (2:15), it says: "So then, brethren, stand firm and hold to the traditions [in Greek, *paradosis*, 'traditions', 'that which is transmitted'] which you were taught by us, either by word of mouth or by letter."

The more I thought about this, the more I realized that the whole idea of Scripture and Tradition meant rather a preservation of the Scriptures, an explanation of the Scriptures, and a protection of the entire revelation, so that it remained intact, authentic, and powerfully operative throughout all of history. During the end of our three years in Israel and more definitively during our time back home in Uppsala, I began to realize that the Catholic Church was the Church instituted by Christ, which held fast to this revelation, to God's Word, when so many newer denominations and movements had let go and allowed the spirit of the age, with all its relativism, to take over.

∽

In Jerusalem, we had come to know many charismatic Catholics. One of them was Kim Kollins, who became a great help to us. She is an American who has worked ecumenically in different communities for many years. She had been an evangelist in the American Word of Faith movement, but she converted to the Catholic Church many years ago. It was nice for us to meet a Catholic who had an understanding of people like us. But we were a little bewildered when upon first meeting us in 2004, she said: "I have waited for you. I see a bridge where many are going forward."

~

In November of the same year, we traveled to Rome to meet her again. Kim wanted to introduce us to Monsignor Usma Gomez and Monsignor Radano at the Pontifical Council for Christian Unity. This secretariat had for many years carried out dialogues with many different churches and denominations, even the American Assemblies of God, which is comparable to the Swedish Pentecostal movement. Kim had a strong wish to show the Pontifical Council for Christian Unity that there is a very large group of Christians who do not belong to the category of the Pentecostal movement/Assemblies of God but, rather, call themselves *nondenominational charismatics*. So, when we were introduced as belonging to a kind of free group of charismatics, who were not classical Pentecostals, a certain confusion arose. They were not completely sure that they understood what we were, and it was not so easy for us to explain. We did as well as we could, and it was a friendly conversation. When we left there, however, my overall impression was that we had only disturbed these gentlemen, and I did not think it would lead any farther. But eventually it did.

After lunch that same day, Birgitta and I walked together with Kim around Saint Peter's Basilica. We began down in the Scavi archeological excavation area, under the basilica itself. It is an old Roman burial site that was hidden under great masses of earth when the Emperor Constantine leveled Vatican Hill in the fourth century and created a solid platform in order to be able to build the first Saint Peter's church. By doing this, the place where, according to tradition, the apostle Peter had been buried after having been crucified upside down just next to the Vatican Hill was also buried under the earth. But the altar in Saint Peter's church was built directly over the place that had been considered to be Saint Peter's grave since the time of the apostles.

It was only in the 1940s that they began to excavate there, and, during the pontificate of Pope Pius XII, they found what was thought to be the original burial place of the apostle Peter. At that time, they, in fact, found some bones in the wall, near a small altar, and this place lies directly under the main altar in the present Basilica of Saint Peter.

I thought it was very exciting to go down to these narrow, underground streets from the Roman era and finally come to what is assumed to be the grave of Saint Peter.

Through an opening, we could see some pieces of bone. And there, before the grave, I was filled with a holy awe. It was totally possible that what we saw was from the body of the apostle Peter! This was extremely fascinating! Here I am, standing before him who had himself touched Jesus. He who had left his nets, followed him, and become a disciple of Jesus. He of whom Jesus said: "And I tell you, you are Peter, and on this rock I will build my Church" (Mt 16:18).

I had myself many times explained away these words of the Bible by saying Jesus meant Peter's confession, not his person. But if one reads carefully, Jesus speaks both to and about him, the apostle Peter himself. Now I stood and looked at what are probably the remains of his earthly body. I trembled. I became mute with awe. A feeling of genuineness, of both authenticity and historicity, came over me. The realization that this was really true, that this apostle was exactly what Jesus had said he would be—Cephas, the rock on which Jesus built his Church—became so concrete and real to me, right then and there.

I felt so small there where I stood and realized that Christ's Church is so great, so far-reaching, so well founded, and, in fact, invincible. All of this went through my mind and welled up in me like a spring of joyful and astonished certainty.

From this burial site, one can walk up a spiral staircase and come up next to the altar in the church itself. Its greatness, its timelessness, its beauty, its openness surrounded me, and I drew in my breath, despite the fact that I had been there many times before. When I saw the altar, with Bernini's spiral columns of copper, I also saw the apostolic historicity that went through the whole history of the Church and out over the whole world. The office and ministry of Peter were truly entrusted to the pope's person and ministry! It was not only a logical thought process; it was something much more. I realized that it was not at all strange that Jesus had appointed Peter as his representative and, thereby, also his successor, as a guarantee of the well-being, unity, and survival of the Church. I also realized that this ministry is truly necessary for the preservation and survival of the Christian faith. As the Church's servant, Peter's office should preserve, in love and humility, the faith, the unity, and the mission to go out into the whole world.

In the Gospel of Matthew 16:18–19, Jesus says clearly to the apostle Peter:

> And I tell you, you are Peter, and on this rock I will build my Church, and the gates of Hades shall not prevail against it. I will give you the keys of the kingdom of heaven, and whatever you bind on earth shall be bound in heaven, and whatever you loose on earth shall be loosed in heaven.

There was no doubt that the office Jesus gave to Peter was very powerful and was meant to last as long as there is a Church. He had said to him "Tend my sheep" (Jn 21:16). This was meant, not for just a few sheep, but for all Jesus' sheep. Was there really a Petrine ministry that stretched through time and, through the mandate given by Jesus, gathered and protected the sheep? I began to realize that it really was so.

I was a bit overwhelmed and thought about this as we walked slowly toward the exit. Then something happened that I cannot explain, nor do I wish to explain it away. We went through one of the gates and came out into the large loggia. We stopped between the great pillars where one can see Saint Peter's Square and the great and beautiful street Via della Conciliazione, which stretches all the way down to the Tiber River. Over Rome's silhouette arched a radiant blue sky. Great flocks of birds flew gracefully back and forth over the housetops and the square. They looked like the jackdaws in the evening hours in Uppsala, when they flew in different formations.

All of a sudden, all these birds gathered together up in the sky and formed themselves into a gigantic exclamation mark, with a tall vertical line and a perfectly rounded point underneath it! All three of us saw this at the same time and just stared with our mouths open. It was so remarkable and like a great confirmation for me, a clear answer to all my question marks. Naturally, it was not as though the sign would be the deciding factor, but it was a very striking event in that particular situation. I also believe it was an expression of God's sense of humor—as though he really wanted to underline what he wished to make known to us with the help of his creation.

～

In April 2005, I was invited to preach in Zagreb, Croatia. The attitude in the congregation I visited was not at all positive toward Catholics, and it did not feel very nice. I spoke with the leaders to point out what was negative about this, but it seemed futile.

When we now found ourselves in Croatia, we wanted to take the opportunity to see Medjugorje, about which we had heard two and a half years earlier. So, after the days in Zagreb, we met together with some friends who would drive us to Medjugorje in the neighboring state of Bosnia. We spent only a day and a night there, but it was an important and enlightening trip.

When we arrived, we went directly to the large church that had been built in that little town. The church was absolutely filled to capacity. There was such a sense of God's presence around the church and the Eucharistic celebration that even on the steps outside, I felt that I must go down on my knees in prayer. And as we stood in the back of the church, we felt we were on holy ground. When one reads about the history around the apparitions in Medjugorje, a Franciscan priest, Father Jozo, is mentioned. He was the one who had protected the children who had seen the Virgin Mary on many occasions. The apparitions took place in 1981 and allegedly have continued since then, and the Yugoslavian Communist police were hard on the Christians who boldly dared to practice their faith.

We had the opportunity to meet Father Jozo briefly and to converse a little with him. We also heard him preach, and I was very impressed with his strong homily, which was about "the two tables", the table of the Word and the table of the Eucharist, and how we must eat from both of these. After the service, he took us into the sacristy and conversed with us and prayed for us. The same day, we were also able to meet one of the visionaries who had seen the Virgin Mary and to speak a little with her. She was, of course, an adult now, but strongly influenced by what she had experienced, and it was interesting to meet her and to hear her tell a little about this. It was obvious for us that there was a great love for the Lord in this place and that many had met Jesus here. It was not possible to deny that thousands of people's lives had been transformed in this place.

This was April 19, 2005, and when we drove back to the youth hostel in Medjugorje after having met Father Jozo, we turned on the radio, and our Italian friends listened eagerly to hear how the conclave was going in Rome. A new pope was to be elected, and our friends hoped that it would be Cardinal Schönborn, who was their favorite among the cardinals. Suddenly the message came: White smoke had been seen in the Vatican's chimney, and soon we and the whole world would know that it was Cardinal Ratzinger who would succeed John Paul II. The new pope had taken the name Benedict XVI.

~

The time in Israel was passing quickly, and we were making many discoveries, even though much of this had not yet been integrated into our lives, but in the spring of 2005, we knew it would soon be time for us to return to Sweden again. Very grateful for those three years in Jerusalem, we returned to Uppsala in the month of May.

In September 2005, Kim Kollins suggested that we should fly over to England so that she could introduce us to Charles Whitehead. For many years, Charles had been the president of ICCRS (International Catholic Charismatic Renewal Services), which is the organization for the Catholic charismatic renewal movement. We flew there and were given a very friendly reception by Charles. Kim talked about the idea that discussions ought to take place between the Vatican and representatives of all nondenominational charismatic Christians. We also met Michelle Moran (who is today the President of ICCRS), her husband, Peter, and other members of the Sion Catholic charismatic community. Flying home to Sweden again, we were very grateful for having met these nice British Catholics.

It was indeed good to meet Charles Whitehead. He and his Anglican wife, Sue, have since then been a great blessing and help to us, and we have had a wonderful fellowship over the years.

We were eventually invited to Rome in March 2007 to participate in a gathering with Catholic and Protestant charismatics who had been meeting for some years. The group went by the name: "Gathering in the Holy Spirit", and the participants came from England, Germany, the United States, and some other nations. Charles and Sue Whitehead, Kim Kollins, and many other leaders, both Catholic and Protestant, participated in these talks. The discussions and the prayers had much to do with the questions of unity and how we could come closer to each other, especially through the charismatic experience of the life and power of the Holy Spirit. Informal conversations were started between the Vatican and nondenominational charismatics in 2008. It was so beneficial to be a part of the group that held these discussions, and I had the joy of writing the papers from the Protestant point of view that were presented at three consultations during the coming years.

For two days, we talked and listened to each other. The Catholic Church, represented by a group that was led by Bishop Brian Farrell, the secretary for the Pontifical Council for Christian Unity, presented their document, and we presented ours. We read together, discussed, and prayed about them. We learned much from each other and had a very good fellowship. Every discussion ended with a written conclusion. This occurred every other year for six years.

To have this chance to cooperate actively in ecumenical talks became very important for me. I had the opportunity both to reflect on my own theological position and to study the Catholic position in greater detail on a number of issues. It became a more penetrating study of our strengths and weaknesses. To have the courage to look at myself from the outside and evaluate where I actually stood theologically on different questions now had become more urgent for me.

Chapter 5

Birgitta: I Really Want to Understand the Role of Mary

In Jerusalem, the environment is filled with beauty, both in the nature God has created and in the culture that the people have built up over the centuries. It is easy to be inspired there, filled with solemnity and reverence.

Ulf and I had the joy of living in a so-called Turkish house in Ein Kerem. This meant that it was built in the old oriental style with walls of stone and an arched ceiling in the living room. In several rooms, we also had old Arabic tile flooring with flower patterns in soft, muted colors. A large terrace with flowerpots faced out toward the hills of Judea. It was peaceful and beautiful. From the valley, we heard the braying of donkeys and sometimes the howling of jackals. The house stood on a steep slope, and we heard the ringing of bells from Saint John Ba'Harim (Saint John in the Mountains) overhead—so near did we live to the birthplace of John the Baptist. A little farther down the road, there was a well that is called Mary's well. Between these two points we had our workplace. Everything lay within walking distance.

Ein Kerem is popular in many respects. Every day, we saw busloads of pilgrims who visited the churches. But even the Israelis flocked there on the Sabbath, since the atmosphere

is nice and feels refreshingly different from Jerusalem itself.
The mountainsides have terraces that go far back before the
time of Jesus. From Mary's well, there is a valley that goes
down toward the main road in the distance, and just there,
up an old path, Mary must have come hurrying to visit
her cousin Elizabeth. It was impossible to avoid thinking of
Mary when one lived in Ein Kerem.

In the fall of 2003, we saw for the first time Saint Mark's
church in the Armenian quarter of Jerusalem. If one is not
familiar with it, it is not easy to find, but it has an exciting
history. Opinions differ about many things in Jerusalem, and
it is the same with this place. It is usually said that the Upper
Room, where Jesus instituted the Eucharist, is located on
Mount Zion, outside the present city wall. But another theory is that the Upper Room is here in Saint Mark's Syrian
Orthodox church. We were met by an Iraqi sister, who told
us this theory and about the history of this church. Then,
suddenly she began singing the Our Father for us in Aramaic,
the language of Jesus. It was so beautiful. She also showed
us an icon of the Virgin Mary with the Child and told us
about completely amazing miracles that had happened when
people prayed through the intercession of Mary. We were
amazed, but we kept silent about our Protestant uncertain-
ties. Could one really pray like this to her?

Some days later when we attended the service at our *kehila*,
the Messianic congregation, there was a visit from a Catholic preacher. His name was Johannes Fichtenbauer, and he is
the archdeacon in Vienna and a close co-worker with Cardinal Schönborn. He preached about "Mary as a model",
and I remember that we thought he was very courageous for
taking up the subject, because the Messianic congregation
is rather evangelical in style and theology.[1] The sermon was

---

[1] A congregation that consists of Jews who believe that Jesus is God's Son.

good and interesting, and we spoke with Johannes the next day. Then we found out that he had known about us since the 1980s, since he was a good friend of Swedes who lived in a community in Vienna. In any case, we liked Fichtenbauer, and over time our paths would cross many times.

Our meeting with Peter Hocken and the Catholic community in Italy occurred around this time, and all these meetings, with such enthusiastic Catholics, gave us much to think about. We were really not prepared for the strong spirituality in the Catholic Church.

An event that was completely awe-inspiring for us was a bishop's consecration in Jerusalem. There are Jewish, Hebrew-speaking Catholics in Jerusalem, and Pope John Paul II decided that the Catholic patriarch of Jerusalem needed an auxiliary bishop at his side, someone who could devote himself especially to them. The pope appointed the Jewish-born French monk Jean-Baptiste Gourion, O.S.B. A good friend took us along to the monastery in Abu Gosh, where Gourion was consecrated bishop on November 9, 2003. Such a solemn occasion! I felt as though I had been transported to the Temple in biblical times, surrounded as I was by incense, liturgical song, beautiful vestments, and crowds of people. The Mass was celebrated by the Arabic Latin patriarch, Bishop Sabbah, and the consecration ceremony was celebrated in Hebrew. It was moving to be present when a Jewish Christian was made bishop in Jerusalem for the first time since the New Testament era. The congregation rejoiced greatly, and people laughed and cried when Bishop Gourion burst out at the end: "Finally we have come back!"

~

What Ulf and I had been zealous about during all the years with the Word of Life congregation was making Jesus known and helping people discover the treasures of the faith and the great riches that are to be found in God's Word. We believed in the necessity of conversion and following Jesus. We believed that he both could and wanted to work miracles today. We also believed that sin and evil not only exist in us people but are also even personified in the one who is called the enemy of souls, Satan. We believed in the power of God's Word and knew that the Lord loves us human beings and died for us on the Cross. We believed that he rose from the dead and that we were all called to proclaim his victory and be his representatives in the world. This was a high calling, and we were so imperfect. But nevertheless, God could and did want to use us.

Over the years, the faith of the Word of Life congregation had been ridiculed in the Swedish press. Our family learned to forgive early on. I remember how I spoke with my children, telling them that not everyone understands that there is a God and that we Christians must forgive and never wish to take revenge. But it is not nice to be singled out and misinterpreted all the time. The good we intend and the holy things in which we believe are distorted and regarded as something wrong and dangerous. The prejudices against us often felt insurmountable and unshakable.

Now, here in Israel, I realized that I was the same way myself. I was judgmental when I came across new expressions of the Christian faith that I did not understand. I was influenced by the Protestant culture in Sweden. The Swedish attitude toward the Catholic Church was that she was something foreign to our culture, southern European and full of curiosities. As both a Lutheran and a free-church Swede, I was also influenced by what was decided at the Reformation. Faith alone. Scripture alone. Grace alone. Preachers and books had warned us about the "heresies" of Rome.

Now I was slowly beginning to see that I was behaving toward the Catholic faith as the media and many in general had behaved toward Word of Life. I was ignorant, and I judged the Church negatively by hearsay. I was ashamed when I realized this. I, who had wished that our opponents at home in Sweden would try harder to find out more about what we really believed—I myself was the same. I believed I knew enough about what Catholics believed about Mary, the pope, and purgatory, but I had not put forth the effort to look into how the Church herself explained and formulated these things. I realized that the Lord wanted to humble me and that it was high time for me to change my attitude. This meant listening to Catholics themselves, their authors and theologians, in order to get a correct idea of their faith.

~

In a short time, we had been able to see many new things, and we had had important experiences. Now it was time for me to come to terms with the theological stumbling blocks that existed between me, as a Protestant, and the Catholic faith.

I had already devoured several books about Saint Birgitta. They awakened many of my questions about Mary and the Catholic dogmas about her. Now I began to read and to try to understand. A book that seemed very suitable for me just at that period was a discussion book about Mary by the authors Longenecker and Gustafson, *Mary: A Catholic-Evangelical Debate*. The Marian dogmas were dealt with here in conversational style, and it was interesting to observe my reactions as I was reading. In the beginning, I was cheering on the evangelical position and thought Gustafson made strong points. The Catholic Longenecker provided good responses, however, and as the discussion progressed, I understood him better and better.

I also read Wilfrid Stinissen's *Mary in the Bible, in Our Life* (*Maria i Bibeln—i vårt liv*). I liked it very much, but at the end of the book, he speaks about the rosary and Mary's intercessory prayer, and I could not really go along with this at that time. I remember how I gesticulated wildly in protest against this in front of Ulf one evening at home. We were missing pieces of the puzzle that we needed in order to be able to understand how Mary could have this role and position.

At the same time, we were working full time. Ulf preached in different congregations in Israel, and we traveled to Armenia, Singapore, and other places. Ulf wrote books, and at this time I remember he was seeking a deeper understanding of the Eucharist and was studying how it had been been celebrated throughout the history of the Church. At the time, Singapore had fantastic bookstores with a good supply of Christian theological books. We bought them by the dozen, yes, even by the barrel.

It is one thing to know about something, and another really to understand it. That the Church is a two-thousand-year-old miracle that God leads and has always watched over is something every Christian ought to know. But an insight that slowly began to grow in me at that time was that the old churches actually carry the precious heritage in a very faithful way, that the way of celebrating the liturgy in the old churches is more like the original than our modern Swedish revival meetings.

There was a theological truth that had never been explained to me properly in my Protestant world. It had to do with Jesus and the Incarnation and Mary's role in this. It was obvious that we believed Jesus is the Son of God, begotten of the Father before time began, conceived by the Holy Spirit, and born of the Virgin Mary here in time. Jesus is God, the second Person in our Triune God. He is the pure Lamb of God who is offered on the Cross in atonement for our sins.

But if he is born of a woman, how can he then escape having a share in the sin that is an inheritance passed down to all of mankind? Certain free churches do not believe in original sin, but we did. This gives rise to a problem: Was Jesus not truly Mary's Son, flesh of her flesh? Yes, of course, all Christians believe this. Through the years, I had heard explanations about how Jesus could be uncontaminated by original sin, but when Ulf and I discussed this, we saw that none of them held up, but, rather, they were often related to early heresies in the history of the Church. The question remained: How can Jesus be free from sin if he is born of a woman out of sinful humanity?

I thought of Uzzah in the story of the Ark of the Covenant in the Old Testament (2 Sam 6:1–13). The Ark was holy and was not to be touched by human hands. But when the Ark moved on a cart that was about to tip over, Uzzah stretched out his hand to prevent it. When he touched it, he died there on the spot. The Ark contained the tablets of the law, the manna, and the staff of Aaron (all three objects that were clearly prefigurations of Jesus), and the people of Israel knew very well that the *shekinah*, God's presence, was there. God had given instructions about how Israel was to handle these holy objects, and in this story, Uzzah breaks the commandments and therefore dies.

So, if God's presence was so tangible in a box of wood and

gold, then how very close is he now, when he comes down and becomes a child inside the womb of Mary? Why does she not die? How does she manage to carry God within her?

I wanted to understand this, and I eagerly read around in Catholic books to find the explanation. Eventually, I found it! When the angel Gabriel came to Mary, he said that she was full of grace. In the Swedish translation from 1917, he says: You are "highly-favored", a beautiful word. What had happened with Mary? What did this greeting mean?

As a Christian, I had understood that for the Incarnation to occur, the woman to give birth to Jesus must have a special grace. But she must also be preserved from the consequences of original sin in order to be God's collaborator in this intimate way, to bear and give birth to God's Son. How was Mary prepared, and when, I wondered?

I read John Paul II's beautiful explanation in his encyclical *Redemptoris Mater* (*Mother of the Redeemer*). Later, I also read how the Catechism explains this mystery. I found the Catechism a treasure that everyone ought to read. Mary is so "highly favored" because God deigned to let her benefit from Jesus' work of redemption already at the moment of her conception. This came as a surprise to me! Like us, she has been redeemed by the blood of Jesus, as Ephesians 1:7 says. But she shared in this grace of salvation beforehand. God, who exists outside of time and space, gave this grace to Mary at her conception because of the mission he had for her. The Child to whom she would give birth, the Savior of the world, was also her Savior. Without him, she would be lost just like us. I quote John Paul II: "The election of Mary is wholly exceptional and unique. Hence also the singularity and uniqueness of her place in the mystery of Christ" (no. 9). He also says: "By virtue of the richness of the grace of the beloved Son, by reason of the redemptive merits of him who willed to become her Son, Mary was *preserved from the inheritance of original sin*" (no. 10, emphasis mine).[2]

When I saw and understood how the Catholic Church explains her election, all the pieces of the puzzle came together regarding this important question. Up to this point, I had believed in the Virgin Birth, and now I could even say I believed in Mary's Immaculate Conception. I was so happy. This had been a great stumbling block, and now it was broken to pieces. When this obstacle was gone, I could see much in the Old Testament that I had never seen before.

When I was young, I had gone for a semester to a Bible school in Uppsala. I had particularly liked a course about prefigurations of Christ in the Old Testament. The Bible is like a diamond and has so many facets. To see all the prefigurations of Jesus in the Old Testament is so fascinating and enriching for one's faith. And now I discovered that even Mary had prefigurations in the history of Israel. So, I continued with my Marian studies in my free time for many years. When I saw the new movie *The Passion of the Christ* that spring, I especially noticed Mary. I could see and understand anew her own painful suffering alongside of her Son.

~

At this point, we had lived in Israel for about one and a half years. Ulf has told about the Catholic community Koinonia and about our new friend Kim Kollins. We really did not know that such people existed: Catholics whose spirituality we recognized but who also had something else that we began to see we really needed. We spoke much with them

---

[2] John Paul II, Encyclical Letter *Mother of the Redeemer* (*Redemptoris Mater*), March 25, 1987. Translation taken from the Vatican website.

about Christian unity and about how it should be manifested.

I especially remember a Mass in Gethsemane garden. I had been in the church there many times, but now we were allowed to go in behind the church, to an old garden with trees and flowers and grottoes. Mass was celebrated there out in the open, and the songs of praise by the young Italians were so beautiful. In my journal, I have written only: "Mass in Gethsemane. My tears were flowing." Yes, tears were flowing, not only because Jesus felt so near, because everything was so beautiful, but also because there is such a great division in the Body of Christ. We ought to be one, but we are not one in a visible way. And this pained me.

~

When the semester was finished, we transported our car over to Greece and then had a wonderful journey home through Europe. Our son Benjamin was with us, and he gave us a tip about San Giovanni Rotondo in Italy and, for us, the relatively unknown monk Padre Pio. Eventually, we would read more about him, but at that time, we were rather ignorant. We then drove farther through the beautiful landscape to the north and saw a little of Rome, Assisi, and Florence. In Germany, we stayed at Darmstadt with the Evangelical Sisters of Mary. I had already heard my father speak of these Sisters and their foundress, Mother Basilea Schlink, with great enthusiasm when I was a teenager, and he had also distributed Mother Basilea's books in the Nordic countries. The Sisters met us with song and much love, and it was wonderful to share their fellowship a little before we traveled on toward home.

At home in Sweden, we continued to work with Word of Life and held conferences in Sweden, Norway, and Finland the whole summer of 2004. It was nice to have a little vacation at our summer cottage and so wonderful to see our children, grandchildren, and our elderly parents. The fact that we made "Catholic discoveries" during those years did not mean that we distanced ourselves from Word of Life. We were only looking for the truth, and the truth belongs to everyone.

~

The fall came, and we traveled back to Israel. When Ulf wrote articles and books, it also involved a great deal of work for me, since I helped him with the proofreading and editing of the texts. It was nice to have workrooms next to each other and to do a great deal of writing together. I was also engaged in the production of Ulf's books and Word of Life's magazine with news from the mission field. I wrote chronicles both for this paper and for the paper *Världen Idag* (The World Today), and we had our great Swedish/Norwegian/Israeli staff that worked with us in the office. We also regularly arranged a pastors' seminar for local Russian Messianic pastors. There are Messianic congregations that consist of immigrant Russian Jews and native Israelis who have come to faith in Jesus throughout the whole country. It was wonderful to get to know these pastors, and they appreciated coming together for fellowship and instruction very much.

In November, Ulf traveled to Singapore to teach at a pastors' course in a church there. He also spoke at an indoor stadium for eleven thousand people. It was inspiring for him, but I did not expect what happened one evening. He

called me from Singapore and told me that he felt like he
had heard an admonition within himself, an appeal to him
saying: "Now is the time for you to get closer to Mother
Church!"

It felt rather astonishing. What did it mean? We loved our
Word of Life congregation and felt a great responsibility for
all the members, close to two hundred thousand people
in our international network in Sweden and in the former
USSR. It was important for us to obey God in the vocation
in which we found ourselves. At the same time, we had to
be sensitive when he wished to teach us something new and
opened new doors. Ulf used to speak with me about the
words that rolled around within him concerning the Catholic Church: discover, appreciate, come close to, and unite
with. We very much wanted to get closer and understand
the Catholic faith better. It became important for us now
to try to break down prejudices in our congregation against
the historical churches. We believed that Word of Life had
so much to gain by seeing the riches that were there.

Only ten days after Ulf heard the inner admonition about
"the Mother Church", we flew together to Rome again. Ulf
has already told about this in a previous chapter, so I do not
need to say more than that I also thought they were exciting
and blessed days. It was a strong experience to walk under
Saint Peter's Basilica in the small passageways from the first
century after Christ and come to what was believed to be
the burial place of Saint Peter. We had always loved Peter
when we read about him in the Bible. He loved his Master,
and Peter's deep regret when he betrayed Jesus is so moving.
And the story of how Jesus restores him that morning after
the Resurrection when they meet again on the shore of the
sea of Galilee is wonderful. We had visited that very place
many times. Today it is called Mensa Christi, and for me

it had become one of the sweetest places to visit in Israel. We had sat there many times in the shade of the large trees and thought of Jesus' words to Peter: Be a shepherd to my sheep, my lambs.

And then we stood there and glimpsed something of his remains, directly under the altar in the huge basilica that bears his name. To come so close to the first among Jesus' apostles was tremendous. There I stood—there he lay—and he had spoken with Jesus face to face. Time and distance seemed to disappear. And then there was that incident with the birds when we left the church . . . Thousands of birds gathering together to form an exclamation mark in the sky. Yes, our whole inner being was just then one single exclamation mark.

~

At home in Israel, we continued our work, but we started to realize that our time there was coming to an end. We were so happy and grateful for our co-workers and friends in the country, but we understood that now we should go back to Uppsala again in the summer of 2005.

I read a few books during that time that meant a great deal to me. Books open windows and sometimes take us outside our own comfort zones. We often need to open the windows and air things out and allow ourselves to be inspired by the saints who have gone before us.

So now I was reading about Faustina, the young nun in Poland who died shortly before the Second World War broke out. Jesus spoke much to her about his great mercy toward sinners, toward all of us. In the midst of very personal sufferings, she wrote down in her diary so many precious things that Jesus revealed to her about his mercy and grace.

Many times she saw Jesus, and she saw that a double stream of love radiates from his heart. Faustina died young, only thirty-three years old, but she was rich in spiritual experiences, and now she is loved throughout the whole world. Her message about Jesus' mercy has helped countless people dare to believe that God loves them.

Another little sister whom I got to know at about that same time was Saint Thérèse of Lisieux. Thérèse was a Carmelite nun and is known for her "Little Way". I read about how she realized she was not able, nor was it necessary for her, to do heroic deeds or "great works" in order to express her love for God. Love is shown in small deeds, and the only way I can show my love is to give every glance and word as an offering of love to the Lord. She saw her own littleness and surrendered herself to Jesus like a little child. One can misunderstand Thérèse and her "childlike" faith and trust, but that total trust and surrender spring from a deep wisdom and theological insight. She is a fascinating person. She also died young; she was only twenty-four years old when she succumbed to tuberculosis in 1897. Since then she has become known and loved throughout the whole world.

These two women challenged me with their humility and their total self-giving love, both for people and for God. What surely moved my heart the most was their burning desire to "save souls", their belief that by intercessory prayer and self-sacrifices they could cry to God for the salvation and eternal wellbeing of mankind. There was much in Catholic piety that was new to me, and I could not understand everything, but I was very attracted by the love, the self-giving, and the perseverance in suffering.

Most people have heard about Saint Francis of Assisi, and we had seen pictures of this little man surrounded by small birds and other animals. I also knew that he was associated with the environmental and peace movements. One could almost think that he was a hippie, born eight hundred years too early.

But then I came across a book about him, *Saint Francis of Assisi*, by Johannes Jørgensen. It was incredibly fascinating for me to get to know him better! He lived a century before Saint Birgitta, so I liked to read about him and get a feeling for the Italy in which Birgitta lived during her last thirty years. I was, of course, humbled and touched by Francis' enormous love for Jesus, his holy life, and his untiring preaching. The fact that he went out to lepers and kissed them and washed their wounds and that he with his own hands repaired churches in disrepair spoke strongly to me of a true disciple of the Lord. I was moved by his great respect for the priestly ministry and Holy Communion, the Eucharist. Once again, I was ashamed of my ignorance and my prejudices. But God is so good, and he leads us gently forward, if we allow him to do it.

When I acquainted myself in peace and quiet with the Catholic faith and its spirituality, I simply had one "aha" moment after another. Many times I thought or said to Ulf: "Why have we not heard this before? Why has nobody told us that this is the way Catholics believe? There is so much that we can assent to with our whole hearts!" I thought that I had seen so many things that everyone in our congregation back home would also be happy to see. Things that we have in common with Catholics. In many questions of faith, we are very close to each other without knowing it!

~

Christmas of 2004, we were home in Uppsala, and it was at this time that the terrible tsunami struck great parts of southeast Asia on the day after Christmas. My brother and his son happened to be there just at that time. It took a while before the rest of the world realized how enormous the catastrophe was, so before we had time to begin to believe that my brother and nephew had been killed, he managed to call us and tell us that they had survived, as though by a miracle. Simon, my nephew, had been lying on a bench on the beach, getting a back massage, and my brother had been sitting near him reading. Just by chance, he had looked up and seen the wave coming on the horizon. The fact that he had then immediately jumped out of his chair and shouted to his son to run had saved their lives. My brother has told and written about those terrible minutes when they rushed upward and heard behind them the roaring and rumbling of the wave. It was as though they were being chased by a wild animal, a devil—even by death itself. I know that God answered our parents' ardent prayers for their son and his family. My father had even said to him before he left on his long trip: "If something dangerous happens, run! Don't turn around!" He must have been inspired by the Holy Spirit to say that, and I am sure that it made my brother act exactly in the right way at the right moment.

~

So we returned to Israel, and we knew this was our last semester in the Holy Land. We enjoyed the beautiful Israeli spring. The valleys around Ein Kerem were filled with almond blossoms, and the brave cyclamen flowers poked their heads out among the rocks together with blood-red poppies.

One day in February, I saw an article in the *Jerusalem Post* with beautiful pictures of a monastery near Bet Shemesh. To my surprise and joy, I realized that this was the monastery that made the beautiful ceramic objects and the Marian figurine that I had bought when we moved to Israel! The monastery is called Beit Jimal and belongs to an Order that is called the Bethlehem Sisters. (Their full name in French is Famille monastique de Bethléem, de l'Assomption de la Vierge et de Saint Bruno.)

I had finally found them! We decided to make an excursion there one Sabbath together with our colleagues. This excursion came to mean an enormous amount to many of us.

We prepared a picnic to eat on the grass, but when we got to the monastery, it began to rain a little, and we took shelter in the nice shop the Sisters had near the entrance gate. We admired the beautiful handmade ceramic objects and the beautiful icons and ceramic figurines. Inside the shop, we met three nuns in white habits and with warm smiles. They were French Sisters, and it was difficult to resist their charm when they offered us delicious small pieces of chocolates that they had made themselves. They invited us to sit in a visiting room and eat our sack lunch, since it was raining. While we ate our lunch, they stayed with us and asked a little about us. We were also curious about who they were and how they lived. So, they asked if we wanted to see their church, and we followed them up the stairs to the roof terrace, where a door led into the loft at the back of the church. We were struck by the devotion in the beautiful limestone church, which had stalls alongside the walls, one for each of the Sisters. Brass lamps hung between the stalls, and rays of light filtered in through the windows' grating. We stood in silence and looked down into the church. A single elderly Sister sat there on a chair below the stairs that led up to the altar. A monstrance stood on the altar, and we understood that the nun was worshipping the Lord in the Sacrament. We had recently read about this and had begun to understand that it was a great and precious treasure. I saw that Avigail, Ulf's secretary, leaned toward the railing of the loft and looked intently at the nun and the monstrance. Tears ran down her cheeks. Ulf also noticed this, and we realized that something had happened in Avigail.

When we came home again to Ein Kerem, Avigail told us that when she saw the Sister before the altar, she saw herself as though in a flash as a little girl at home in the United States. She had grown up there with a Catholic mother, and when she was little she had loved the nuns and dreamed about one day becoming one of them. But in her early teens, she had left her faith and lived many years without contact with her Christian faith, until she had had a renewed experience of God when she was thirty years old, but this time in a Baptist setting. She went along on different paths and eventually ended up with Word of Life in Uppsala. She had suppressed her Catholic background and instead asserted that one of her parents was also a Jew. This drew her to Israel, and after two years of Bible school in Uppsala, she emigrated to Israel. When we eventually moved there, we had met her again, and she became our secretary.

Ulf and I were deeply attracted by what we had seen and experienced at this place. We had already met nice nuns in Jerusalem in different contexts, but these were nuns who lived in a cloister. The Bethlehem Sisters are inspired by the Carthusian Order and live in prayer and in silence. The Sisters had told us that they only recreate and speak with each other on Sunday after Mass. Then they take long walks and talk and laugh together. The Sisters whom we had met were assigned, for a certain amount of time, to taking care of the guests who came to the shop.

It took only a few days before we returned to Beit Jimal. We wanted to take part in Vespers. Now we experienced something particularly beautiful. The liturgy follows a more oriental style, since they live in the Middle East. The songs were sung in French, Hebrew, Arabic, and Latin, and when they worshipped, they did it with their whole bodies. They often bowed down deeply in worship, and at Mass we saw how at times they lay prostrate with their foreheads to the floor. We were moved by the holiness and reverence of the Sisters' worship.

On this second visit, we were also able to speak a little with the Sisters we had met the first time. They told us that they consider Mary as the Foundress and Abbess of all their monasteries. They have a good thirty monasteries spread out in many countries. When they spoke about Mary having such an active role in their lives, we found it a little hard to accept. Were they not mixing Mary up with the Holy Spirit, we wondered? But we did not let that question be an obstacle to our fellowship; rather, we saw that the Sisters were completely wonderful servants of God, from whom we had much to learn.

The idea grew with unexpected quickness in Avigail that she herself was called to monastic life. I really wondered if she was not being too hasty, since I knew her to be such an outgoing person. She loved to evangelize and teach, and she was the type who enjoyed talking and laughing. How would she be able to manage in a monastery like this, I wondered?

～

Even this last spring in Israel meant a good deal of work-related trips for us. We flew to Singapore again, and on such long trips one always needs a good book to read. This time I read *Rome Sweet Home* by Scott and Kimberly Hahn. In a fun and interesting way, they tell about their discovery of the truth and the depths of the Catholic Church. They were Presbyterians, and Ulf and I, with our Protestant background, could understand them and their experience very well. We appreciated reading about how they tackled the theological questions, and I felt that we understood them. But we would not be able to convert like they had. We were in a position of leadership for a great movement with a couple of hundred thousand people who looked up to Ulf as their spiritual leader much as Christians in other churches look up to a respected bishop. We could not abandon all these people.

But we were seeking Truth with a capital T. One may not abandon the Truth, either. We prayed much during these years for God's help and guidance to understand his word correctly and his will for us and Word of Life. Later in the spring, Ulf and I spent a few days in silence at Beit Jimal. We each had our own room and could read, pray, and participate in the services of the Sisters up in the choir loft. They were beautiful days, and I read at that time the fantastic book *Evangelical Is Not Enough*, by the author Thomas Howard. Howard grew up as an evangelical, in a free church, and he speaks in the book with feeling and love for the warm faith of his youth. But he longed for what was historical and authentic, for what had been part of the Church for two thousand years. I recognized myself in his desire for the historical, for what went back to the time of the early Church. Both Ulf and I wanted to learn more about how the liturgy had been celebrated down through the ages. In a clever way, Howard brings up questions about Mary, the sacraments, and other crucial questions, and it was not hard to be convinced that he had found something that was true and right.

Since we lived in Israel, we followed the news on CNN and the BBC. It was the spring of 2005, and Pope John Paul II was very sick. Surely in Sweden we would hardly have been able to follow the news about the condition of the pope as well as we could here. We had come to know this man too late. Ulf had read a thick book about his life and told me much about it, and we had seen two excellent films about his life. "Too late have I loved Thee", wrote Saint Augustine in his *Confessions* in the fourth century, directing those words to Jesus. After a life of sin, he had come to believe, and he grieved deeply that he had taken so long before he responded to God's grace. When the pope was dying, we felt something similar—it was so tragic that only at the end of his life did we realize what a spiritual giant he was. We united ourselves in prayer with all the Catholics in the world for the pope in his last struggle. He died then on April 2. We were at home in Sweden at that time, due to the fact that Ulf's mother had suddenly died. So that day was extra heavy for Ulf, since it was also the day of his dear mother's funeral.

Ulf has already told about our short trip to Medjugorje in Bosnia, so I do not need to do so. But it was two weeks after Pope John Paul II's death, somewhere in the mountains in Bosnia, that we heard on the car radio that Joseph Cardinal Ratzinger had been elected as the new pope. It was wonderful to share with Catholics, for the first time, the excitement and drama surrounding the election of a pope.

Everything we had experienced during these years meant a great deal to us. Full of the new knowledge that we had received during our three years in Israel, we returned to Sweden and our congregation in Uppsala.

Chapter 6

Ulf: Back in Sweden with New Questions

In the summer of 2005, it was time to return to Sweden. The Word of Life work continued in Israel, but we ourselves came back to Uppsala, and I went back to serving as head pastor in the congregation. Many were enthusiastic that we were back, and I perceived that some wished everything to be as it had been before we left for Israel. The eagerness was mixed with a little disappointment, however, when I began to preach about what I had discovered during the past years regarding the great importance of Christian unity. This was something that had captured my heart so completely, and it became ever more important for me to teach about it as well.

Certain people did not think that it was especially important to emphasize unity. But others were glad about the broadening that was now taking place within Word of Life and really wanted to see more of it. We were all tired of being labeled as a sect, which the media had repeatedly done for years. I was convinced that this desire for broadening and deepening and for more fellowship with other Christians was the way for the future.

The desire to go deeper in my understanding of the faith

had to do with my personal spiritual life, but it was also a desire for a deeper dogmatic understanding. I wanted to have a clearer picture of the process of Church history, which led all of us Christians to where we are today. Above all, I wanted to know why we had become estranged and how we could come close to each other again.

That meant that I began to teach more and more about the history and development of the Christian faith. This was a discovery process for me just as much as for the congregation. I simply shared what I had discovered step-by-step, and I myself did not have all the answers or final conclusions at hand. Nor did I have, as some later claimed, a hidden agenda in this. No, I shared what I gradually became convinced of myself. What I had not been convinced of, I continued to ponder and study.

It was that simple. I did not know where my searching and studying would lead. What was impelling me was the desire to discover the greatness in the Body of Christ, the Church, and the spiritual riches that have been deposited in this Body. I also thought of what we were missing in Christianity in different ways, due to the divisions that had arisen throughout history. I began to see all the more clearly that the things we were missing in our own church setting was just what we really needed in order to go forward.

Before we left Israel, I had had time to write a little book about the Eucharist, *Take, Eat*, which attracted some attention. Many liked it, while others were somewhat skeptical about what they thought was a more Catholic position. Regardless, the Eucharist had been growing in importance for me for many years, and the insight about what it actually is was in the process of deepening within me. While pondering the meaning, substance, and function of the Eucharist, I came to understand and affirm more and more that which is

called sacramental theology. In it I found the key to understanding not only the Eucharist but also even the essence of
the Church. Gradually my question about what the essence
of the Church actually is was being answered.

For a typically Pentecostal-charismatic Christian, there is
a great abyss to bridge to understand what a Catholic Mass
is actually about and why certain moments are so important.
Here two different worlds collide.

Birgitta and I had a certain experience of the liturgy
from our past among high-church Lutherans in the Swedish
church. But the majority of those with whom we worked
lacked this experience. Those who came from a more traditional Pentecostal environment often found Catholic litur-
gies and traditions to be completely foreign. Many of them
have, since their early childhood, heard about how wrong
all these things are; the Reformation freed us from all this,
and yet it still lives on in the Catholic Church! To dare
to come closer to a Catholic environment with this background demands a great self-mastery, and I must say that I
can both understand those who do not wish to come closer
and admire those who dare to do so.

For believers in a free-church milieu, the traditional, liturgical service is perceived as rigid and formal and therefore
a dangerous way to go; one wants in every way to guard
freedom in the church service. In the free churches, there
has always been a deeply rooted skepticism about rules that
are too fixed—hence suspicion toward liturgy. One is afraid
that it will prevent the free flow of the Spirit and spontaneous
communication and will thereby also "grieve the Spirit of
God". I could relate to this concern, which I myself had
shared to a certain degree. But now I had started to understand more what the Eucharist actually consisted of and was
about. I myself had never accepted the merely symbolic view

of either baptism or the Eucharist, but there was no doubt about the fact that it was the more symbolic view that prevailed in the environment where I was ministering.

In the beginning, I did not experience this opposition as being so serious but, rather, viewed it as more of a pedagogical challenge. But it gradually became more serious. I realized that the dividing line was much more profound than I had first thought. The dividing line went between those who understood the Christian life to be sacramental and those who did not. It makes a great and decisive difference if Jesus is truly present in the Eucharist or not and if baptism is only an "act of obedience", as many free-church members say, or if the Spirit is truly given to the one who is baptized.

I thought that it was important to introduce a deeper and more biblical understanding of the Eucharist in Word of Life, to increase the number of times the Eucharist was celebrated, and to create a more formal ritual surrounding the Eucharist that accentuated the meaning of Christ's true presence in the bread and wine. This was received with open hearts by many who experienced the communion services as spiritually rich and as something that blessed them in a deeper way. For them, this now became more living and meaningful. The fact that communion now took a more central place allowed many to meet Jesus in a new way.

This had to do with a discovery of true sacramentality. I realized that for many, the word "sacramentality" was the same as some form of magic or superstition. They turned away from what was believed to be a kind of formal, mechanical way of having a church service. But actually they were in fact turning away, often unconsciously, from the real objective content and meaning of the sacraments. This was something I now began to understand. Revivalist-movement

Christianity is based on experience, and preferably on personal, subjective, emotional experiences. It has to do with the need for, and experience of, a personal encounter with Jesus. The personal faith and the personal encounter with Jesus overshadow everything else, which in comparison is considered less significant. The subjective experiences are seldom associated with the means of grace. One prefers not to use the word "sacrament", since it leads one's thoughts to something seen as merely mechanical, formalized, and therefore foreign.

In this environment—which also has much good in itself —it was naturally a smaller revolution to begin to pray fixed and written prayers in connection with the communion service. A few protested, but others experienced a new strength in this. It appeared, in fact, that many longed for forms that were a little more fixed, as long as they saw that they were biblically based. It therefore became a positive discovery for many to see that Jesus himself in fact prayed written prayers at regular times—when he recited the psalms, for example. It was also a discovery to see how both Jesus and the apostles kept themselves within the framework of Jewish liturgical life, both in the Jewish synagogue and in the Temple. During the time of the early Church, the believers kept following the example of Jesus with set times for the prayers from the psalms three times a day in the Temple. When they no longer had access to the Temple, they continued nevertheless to pray in this way. The early Church was not a loosely organized charismatic prayer group of the modern sort; rather, it had fixed forms in the life of prayer, in the liturgical life, and in the leadership. This did not seem to hinder the action of the Spirit at all, as is clearly seen in the Acts of the Apostles.

For me and for many others, it was a discovery and a

liberation to see how the Spirit and the Church, just like the spirit and body, really belong together and how life in fact fills the body and is dependent on a body in order to have a form. The model is Jesus himself, who was anointed by the Holy Spirit and who walked about and preached and worked miracles. He performed these miracles through his body, his mouth, his hands, the hem of his garment, and so on, and he showed in this way how the Church should function. The early Church continued then to act in the same way through the same Spirit. Form in itself is not the problem and need not be a hindrance to faith and spiritual life at all. On the contrary, spiritual life is protected by a form given by God. God has blessed and made holy his physical creation existing in time and space. The problem arises if there is no life, if faith is not there. The hindrance is hardness of the heart, our pride, our unwillingness, and our own unbelief, not the forms in and of themselves.

The early Church had such an obvious and tangible realism in her view of the sacred rituals and actions. They were more than just symbols. They also *mediated* what they represented. Many for whom I preached began to realize that the merely symbolic view of baptism and communion did not measure up. All of a sudden, the Incarnation had a still clearer meaning. We knew that Jesus was not only a spirit but that he truly had a physical form. Jesus, who is true God, became true man of flesh and blood. When he spoke about salvation and his Kingdom, he also spoke about water, bread, and wine as means for God's action in a very realistic way. As "Bible-believing Christians", we wanted to be faithful to the words of the Bible. But when it came to the Eucharist and baptism, the words of the Bible seemed very challenging.

In the Gospel of John 6:53–54, Jesus says:

Truly, truly, I say to you, unless you eat the flesh of the
Son of man and drink his blood, you have no life in you;
he who eats my flesh and drinks my blood has eternal life,
and I will raise him up at the last day.

In the Gospel of Matthew 26:26–28, it says:

Now as they were eating, Jesus took bread, and blessed, and
broke it, and gave it to the disciples and said, "Take, eat;
this is my body." And he took a chalice, and when he had
given thanks he gave it to them, saying, "Drink of it, all of
you; for this is my blood of the covenant, which is poured
out for many for the forgiveness of sins."

Here Jesus says in an extremely clear way that the bread
and the wine of the Eucharist are his body and his blood.
He says what he means, and he means what he says.

In regard to the Eucharist, it was difficult for many in
our movement to admit readily that Jesus actually meant exactly what he said. When he said this the first time, he was
thought to be so radical that many stopped following him,
since they could not tolerate hearing such "hard words".
But what he says is that if we want to have eternal life, we
must eat of his body and drink of his blood.

This insight overwhelmed me. Before, I had more or less
automatically assumed, in the typical evangelical spirit, that
in his preaching in chapter six of the Gospel of John, Jesus
meant the Word when he said bread, since God's Word is
food for us, according to the Gospel of Matthew 4:4. But
that is not what he says here. He speaks unmistakably about
his own flesh and blood, about his imminent atonement,
and how he lets himself become food for us every time we
celebrate the Holy Eucharist in memory of him.

All of a sudden, I realized that what characterized me in
relationship to the Eucharist and to other means of grace

was not faith, but unbelief! I did not believe that it was truly Jesus' body and blood. I did not believe that the water of baptism truly transmitted rebirth by the Holy Spirit, despite the fact that Jesus says so in the Gospel of John 3:5–6, the apostle Paul says it in the Letter to Titus 3:5, and the apostle Peter says it in 1 Peter 3:20–21. My somewhat self-assured but nonetheless selective faith in the Bible received a strong blow, and I felt as though Jesus were reproaching me for my heart's unbelief and hardness. Now I saw my unwillingness to believe that it is truly just as he says; that he communicates his grace, which we are able to receive in faith, through the physical means that he chose. It was in this way salvation came to us, through the Incarnation. It was in this way that he worked miracles among us on earth, when he used his spittle, the hem of his garment, or the water in the Pool of Siloam. And it was about this that he spoke when he instituted the Eucharist.

I had sensed this sacramental dimension but had not really understood it. Now I seriously started to realize what an asset it is for us Christians. Jesus comes to us in a concrete way through the sacraments. They are external, physically visible means through which God communicates his inner, invisible, tangibly present grace to us. He does it because he has bound his word and his promises to these means. These external signs—water, bread, wine, oil, and the laying on of hands—both represent God's grace and communicate the grace they represent. This insight was almost overpowering.

I did not actually need to know more to understand what an immensely great blessing and gift this is. I realized that this is something that the Church has believed down through the ages and that I must assent to this historical faith deeply in order to be a credible Christian myself. I could not simply pick and choose among different truths and sift out what I did not like. It was as though I saw Christ on the Cross, when water and blood poured out in order to give us life. I could now see the Church as a great reservoir, with endless rivers of grace flowing through different channels for different times and needs in our lives. We can and should drink of this grace daily.

I realized how it must grieve Jesus when we do not want to partake in the sacramental life of the Church. I literally thirsted and hungered more and more for this reality. On one occasion, I felt it was as though I found myself outside a bakery with delicious pastries inside but with a glass windowpane that separated me from them. I could see but not taste. I would have to step inside and sit down . . . , but I had not yet come that far.

This insight into the blessing of the sacraments does not mean that the Word takes a lesser place, that one cannot pray spontaneous, personal prayers, that the charismatic gifts of grace are no longer real or necessary. No, the Church is both sacramental, evangelical, charismatic, diaconal, and so much more, in accordance with the fullness that exists in her. Now I seriously began to discover the Church.

～

In the wonderful fellowship we had for so many years with Word of Life, so much of our work consisted of church planting and church development. After having been brutally criticized for many years, Word of Life became more and more recognized as the years went by, not the least through our far-reaching missionary work. Several hundred new churches had come into being in Russia, the Ukraine, and other nations, and the missionary work was wonderful and exciting. There is hardly anything more satisfying than to come to a place—Russia, the Baltic countries, Armenia, or Albania—where people have not yet heard, at least not in this generation, the Gospel of Jesus and then to be able to preach about him there. To see these people—often young but even old and graying—give their lives to Jesus is so precious. What a joy it was to be able to do an evangelist's work in these countries during the special time that followed the fall of the Iron Curtain.

Through this missionary work, with the help of our books and videos as well as visits by many evangelists, new congregations had begun to form. They often arose spontaneously, and we came there to help them find structure and Bible teaching. These smaller and larger congregations, which one could find in the mountains of Central Asia or out in the middle of the Siberian tundra, were truly fascinating. Our missionaries traveled everywhere. Many of them lived there for several years, often under great hardship. Rather soon, the question of leadership became very important, and the need for leadership training was acute. It was difficult to keep up with this quick growth, and the hunger for God's Word was very great everywhere.

~

The question about the sacraments was naturally important for the new congregations in our mission fields as well as at home in Sweden, since it is a question of grace being transmitted in the right way. When I thought about this, the question regarding *authentic authority* in relationship to doctrine and the administration of the sacraments also came to the fore. This question is related to a correct view of *historicity*. What is the Church of Christ on earth and how is she best represented in her fullness? How was Christ's Church founded on earth, and is there a continuity that is valid even up to this day? I asked myself how all these newly formed congregations that we had started stood in relation to the rest of the Body of Christ. In the beginning of our missionary work, these questions were absent, due to the Pentecostal-charismatic model we had adopted, in which the congregations are independent and autonomous. But step-by-step, the questions began to be more persistent. Personally, I saw ever more clearly what was available for our benefit in Christian history.

I believe that when Protestant Christians open themselves to see the work of the Spirit in the Church throughout history, a temptation to become eclectic can quickly present itself. That would mean arbitrarily picking and choosing for ourselves what we like in what we have discovered in the Church Fathers and the early Christian tradition. At the same time, we push to the background what we do not appreciate or what we think is too foreign or controversial. We are tempted to put on a kind of costume and play Church on our own terms, as if to reinvent the wheel.

For some time it had been this way for me. It was a little easier, and perhaps at a certain period also necessary, to bring out things from the storehouse of the Church and then try to incorporate them into our own context. But I began to be more doubtful about this way of acting. Can one really speak about bishops (as our congregations in Russia began to do) without, at the same time, assenting to how the early Church looked upon the office of bishops? Can one celebrate the Eucharist as it was in the early Church without sharing in the Offices that were recognized by the early Church? Can one quote the Church Fathers only when they say what one already agrees with but ignore the rest?

Am I not then taking only what I prefer and overlooking the context?

I began to reflect on the Church's *apostolicity and authenticity* more and more. In other words: I wondered how one could know that one had true apostolic teaching and a correct apostolic praxis. How do we know that we are a biblical, apostolic church? Are there really many different churches?

We knew, of course, that we were Christians. We loved the Lord Jesus Christ, believed in him, and wanted to follow him. We believed in God's Word and preached the Cross, atonement, and the forgiveness of sins in the power of the blood of Jesus. We preached justification by grace through faith. We proclaimed the reality of new birth through conversion and the Spirit's indwelling in the hearts of believers. All of this was good and based on God's Word. Nevertheless, it felt as if elements were missing, and I pondered over what they were. Were there things that we had lost through the division that exists in the Body of Christ, a division we, too, were guilty of deepening?

These questions came to the surface through the experience I had of new congregations in Sweden but even more through the establishment of all the new congregations in our mission fields. With a rather informal view of the Church, an ecclesiology that was not developed and that was very pragmatically inspired, we did indeed simplify things. And it also looked like this approach worked well on many of our mission fields. People heard the Gospel and came to faith in Jesus Christ. We worked hard, and I was totally focused on and occupied with the instruction and training of pastors by means of the many seminars and courses for pastors that we quickly organized. (These courses for pastors, held for thousands of leaders in many countries, were the precursors to the more formal, pastoral education that we carried out in the administration of Word of Life University.)

This work took up much of my time, of course, and involved much traveling. The new churches that we had started were a result of the charismatic preaching and the spiritual life we tried to pass on. A congregationalist perspective, with free, more or less independent parishes, characterized the preaching. These parishes were led by a senior pastor and his assistant. It was a simple and often very functional model, which in the beginning stages brought about quick growth through flexibility and minimal bureaucracy.

But after a few years, problems occurred. Who actually decided who would become the pastors? What kind of organization would the different parishes have, and who settled disputes? Who decided the content of the teaching and how? When a strong charismatic movement lands in the concrete situation of building up a parish, many questions arise. These questions cannot be answered merely by referring to the inner guidance of the Spirit in every individual pastor's or member's heart. Nor are the new concrete questions that come up unimportant; rather, they must be resolved in such a way that there is unanimity between the different parishes. And then we had the question of discipline. If a pastor committed adultery or misused his position to his own advantage, who would then have the genuine authority to admonish, discipline, stop, or rehabilitate the pastors who had misbehaved?

The congregationalist, independent, free-church model gave much authority to the individual parish, which worked excellently when everything functioned well. It gave room for a multitude of different initiatives on the grassroots level. But what happened if the pastor or a whole parish went astray? Was there then a legitimate authority that could come

in from the outside and help these churches reform themselves? There were definite weaknesses here and examples
of pastors and parishes that in crises did not listen to anyone
from the outside. In the reality in which I lived during that
time, these questions became very important. Many pastors
were very eager to receive advice, instruction, and encouragement from a leader. But far fewer were as eager to receive
advice if opinions differed. In the end, the individual pastor
did, nevertheless, what he himself thought best; he was the
final and highest authority. Questions about influence and
authority versus serving the members, about setting an example by living a holy life, and about being open and trans-
parent became very pressing and real. While in the beginning, the missionary work dealt mostly with fundamental
knowledge about the Bible, prayer, the gifts of the Spirit
and evangelization, as years went by, completely different
questions began to become more urgent.

~

This process of change motivated me to begin to search
for genuine and lasting answers to these important questions concerning church development. I found the answers
in how the early Church had developed, which led me to
ponder increasingly the question of where this Church actually exists today. My important experience in Ein Kerem
with the dead olive tree that was not dead at all echoed
within me and gave rise to many questions.

Where was the stability and continuity? Was it true that
there was a genuine, noble olive tree—the Church tree—
whose roots went all the way back to the time of Jesus?
Was it true that the wheel, the Church, did not need to be

reinvented in every generation? Is continuity more important than spontaneous, spiritual movements? Was it true that
with every new division in the Church—including the one I
myself had initiated—the new movement that developed did
not become automatically stronger but, rather, with time,
became instead weaker, more diluted, and more impover-
ished? We so eagerly wanted to believe the opposite, that it
became more original and thereby purer and stronger.

Was it even the case that I had contributed to more secularization, not less? Did our all too pragmatic position, concentrated as it was on practical matters, lead to the fact that
certain questions—for example, about the gifts of the Holy
Spirit, healing, and miracles—overshadowed other important questions? The risk of an all too specialized development became clear.

Now the questions began to become serious and even
worrying. I also began to see signs of different forms of
compromise and worldliness within the so-called revivalist Christianity. I had already read the Catholic priest Peter
Hocken's book *The Glory and the Shame* in Israel, and we
published it at Word of Life's publishing company. This
book gave form to my thoughts. I continued to think along
these lines, which made it possible to accept and affirm the
good that exists within Pentecostal-charismatic movements
while, at the same time, becoming more open to what the
historical, and above all the Catholic, Church actually stood
for and had to offer.

This could be summed up in three concepts I have already
mentioned. The first was *historicity* in a time when Christians were becoming less historically oriented and despised
the past. I saw that much of revivalist Christianity was a
reaction to something in the past and therefore had found

its identity in constantly distancing itself from other groups or older churches. These attitudes were counterproductive. They led only to more and more elitism and sectarianism.

The second was *authenticity* in a time of quite a few rather sensational and spectacular manifestations and claims in the modern Christian world. Individual pastors traveled around or appeared on Christian television with the most unbelievable claims. Some of them seemed to commercialize the conception of revival and the spiritual life. In contrast stood what was authentic: the soundness, the genuineness, the simplicity, and the thoroughness of the Catholic faith.

The third was *authority* in a time when most of us basically only obeyed ourselves. Where was a legitimate teaching office and a genuine pastoral ministry that stood in sound relationships to other ministers? Could anyone at all really come forth and make the claim to be a leader, pastor, evangelist, or prophet only with the reference that "God had spoken to him"? The Catholic Church's view of the teaching office was for me a healthy counterbalance to an individualistic and arbitrary interpretation of the Bible.

The more I studied and reflected on this, the more I realized that the Catholic Church not only had important and well-considered answers to these questions. *She was the answer.* I realized that what the Catholic Church actually *is*, not only what she does, was the solution to a multitude of questions and problems with which Protestantism struggled in its many different forms and expressions.

More and more, I began to realize that it was not enough to collect spiritual knowledge and experience from different time periods and then merely try to integrate them into our own work. There was something that was missing, not only in different spiritual experiences, expressions, and forms, but also in the very foundation of our understanding of the

Church. What is it, where is it, and how is it in its fullest and most genuine expression?

Time after time, a thought came back to me—each time ever more pressing. They were the words I had heard inside of me already in the fall of 2004 and which at that time had perplexed me: "Come closer to Mother Church."

Chapter 7

Ulf: Saints, Miracles, and Important Meetings

With all these new theological questions that I was turning over in my mind, the journey of discovery continued in different ways. There was so much more to learn, books to read, places to visit, and people to meet. I became aware of the accuracy and logic in Catholic theology and appreciated the fact that reason was not underestimated but was rather placed clearly in God's service. But the Christian life is not only theology and Bible studies; it is above all communion with people who have been touched and transformed by God. Meeting spiritually alive Catholics and reading the dramatic stories of the saints made a strong impression on me.

When we had the opportunity, we sought out historical places to find out more about what had happened there and why. In many places and in the lives of many saints, very tangible miracles had occurred. The saints often suffered and were misunderstood during their lifetimes, but they did not leave the Church and "start their own". Rather, they lived their lives in communion with the Church and were a great blessing to her.

One person whom our son Benjamin brought to our attention was the Italian Franciscan Brother Padre Pio. I had never heard of him before, but I was very impressed when I read about his complete surrender to Jesus and all the miracles that had been linked to him. An exciting book by Bernard Ruffin, *Padre Pio, the True Story*, captivated both Birgitta and me.

It was during the summer of 2004 as we drove home to Sweden and traveled through Italy that Benjamin persuaded us to take the road past San Giovanni Rotondo, where Padre Pio had lived the greater part of his life. When we got there, the little town was swarming with people. We visited his grave and the church where he had celebrated Mass. We also saw the large hospital complex that he, by his faith, had built. It was impressive.

Padre Pio lived from 1887 to 1968 and was an incredibly special person who drew people from around the world, not least of all by hearing confessions and praying for the sick. He was blessed with many of the charismatic gifts about which Saint Paul speaks in the First Letter to the Corinthians (12) and had an unusual ability to see into other people's souls and know their problems. Padre Pio had many strong spiritual experiences and, among other things, received the stigmata; that is, he received the wounds of Jesus in his body in a supernatural way. Up to now, I had been skeptical about such things, but after having read how carefully he was examined, I had little doubt that he really did have these inexplicable wounds. He bore the marks of Christ's wounds for all of his adult life, and they caused him much pain. (See the Letter to the Galatians 6:17, where Saint Paul says, "I bear on my body the marks of Jesus.") I had to change my opinion about this, as about so many other things, and I realized that Jesus can very well allow a person to bear the marks of his Passion in his body as a sign and reminder of his work of atonement. Padre Pio's long life was filled with suffering, intercessory prayer, and a very real battle with Satan. But it was also filled with ecstasy, visions, and extraordinary miracles. Naturally, during his lifetime he was very controversial because he consented so concretely to the supernatural aspects of the faith. Many theologians did not like this at all, in contrast to the grateful people who sought after him.

Birgitta has related how we came in contact with the Bethlehem Sisters in Beit Jimal outside of Beit Shemesh in Israel in February 2005 and how our secretary was moved by their devotion. She was also rather soon received as a novice among them. The Bethlehem Sisters' devotion was so palpable and so beautiful in its expressions. Their joy was striking, and their love for Jesus was all-pervasive and disarming. When one came there, it was as though one were showered with a holy purity. Experiencing their prayer life was like coming into a spiritual nuclear power plant. We became very good friends with them, and the contact with them—intense, decisive, and beneficial—has continued since then. It is always a joy to see them again. Their prayers and wise counsel have followed us in all the recent phases of our journey.

It has been particularly special to go there with busloads of passengers on the Word of Life tours to Israel. Sometimes we had people with us who had never been to a Catholic monastery and who were so skeptical that they would hardly get out of the bus, much less set foot inside the monastery door. When they finally came in with us, it was truly moving to see how taken they were by the witness of the nuns and by the love they radiated. Very many had a completely changed view of both nuns and the Catholic Church after their visit there. During the following years, we were able to take about two thousand pilgrims with us to visit them.

Through these Sisters, we also came in contact with other

places where they worked. One such place was Lourdes in southern France, a pilgrimage site that I had heard about when I was in school. It was said that the Virgin Mary had appeared there in 1858 to a young girl named Bernadette, after which miracles and healings had occurred. That was about as much as I knew, and I was skeptical. The idea that the Virgin Mary could appear was completely foreign to me; in school we had learned that such manifestations bordered on the occult. It ought to be Jesus and no one else who revealed himself!

But in the Bible, I read how angels came to visit the Virgin Mary and visited Joseph in a dream. An angel came and freed Peter from his chains and opened the prison gate for him. An angel stirred up the waters in the Pool of Siloam so that people could be healed by going down into the water. The prophet Samuel came to King Saul after his death and warned him. And both Moses and Elijah appeared together with Jesus to the disciples on the mount of the Transfiguration. There were biblical examples of holy people and angels who had come with messages directly from the heavenly world.

I remember that for years I had wondered why the Lord sent angels instead of speaking directly to his people. Remembering now the many biblical examples where the Lord spoke and acted in different ways, I realized that the Lord could naturally also send his own Mother as a messenger if he willed. And when I investigated the apparitions at Lourdes a little more closely, I saw that they only pointed to him and glorified him—just as Mary did at the wedding feast at Cana. It is, in fact, the content of the message and who is glorified by it that determines if it is authentic or not.

It is something totally different to try to conjure up the dead with occult magic, which the Bible clearly forbids.

The saints who have fallen asleep in God's grace now live in prayer and praise before God, and in the Letter to the Hebrews 12:23, they are called an "assembly of the first-born" of God, the righteous who have been "made perfect". They are alive to the highest degree, more living than we are here on earth, and they live constantly before God and are perfected in his will.

~

In my life as a Christian, I have always considered the supernatural life and miracles to be something important. To read the Bible and follow Jesus through the Scriptures is to come into contact with the supernatural. The Gospel is not only about what Jesus said and what we ought to do; it is also about all the miracles Jesus did for us human beings and about the transformations that happened through his intervention. Or are the miracles that the Evangelists describe really myths? Or did he truly do these things then, but not anymore?

These are important questions that touch upon what is central in our Christian faith: who Jesus really is and what the essence of the Church, which is his Body, really is. Miracles are not only about a superficial desire for something spectacular or quick solutions to difficult problems; rather, they are the foundational claim of the Christian faith. Our faith is in its essence supernatural.

As a young theology student, I found it tiresome to have to listen constantly to exegetical attempts to explain away Jesus' miracles. It is certainly true that the Bible contains many dimensions and that there are different literary genres that one must consider in order to understand its message correctly. But when the conclusion was reached that, in

principle, we could not know much or even anything about
the historical Jesus and therefore had to dismiss his miracles
as later additions and constructions, I found that difficult to
accept. And when modern exegetes chisel away layer upon
layer of what is thought to be tradition, myths, popular be-
liefs, an antiquated world view, and later additions to the
text, in the end there is not much left to believe in or rely
upon. When the conclusion is reached that these miracles
did not in fact happen or that it is not at all necessary for
them to have a historical anchoring in reality in order to
believe in Christ, then it easily becomes absurd. In all ages,
but not the least in our own time, the supernatural aspect
of the Christian faith has been questioned and challenged.
That is why it was so refreshing to discover that the Catholic
Church, sometimes against all odds, has always held fast to
the supernatural. Once again, I was struck by how Catholics
believed *more*, not less, and how we Protestants often came
with rationalistic objections.

Irrespective of the origin of the Bible's history and the
fact that there are different dimensions in the texts that give
room for deep symbolism, the Church has always believed
that the drama of salvation really took place in time and
space in our world. The holy text of the Bible, such as it
has been transmitted to us by the Church, is credible and
clearly remains a guide in our lives.

Simply expressed: Jesus worked real miracles, with real
people, at definite times, and in real places when he walked
on this earth. His miracles were signs that had different dimensions and symbolism, but they really happened. The
one does not exclude the other. The Resurrection of Jesus
was the greatest miracle and a unique, unparalleled historical event that transformed everything.

God can and still wants to work miracles of different

kinds, even for us today. That the Catholic Church has always held fast to the supernatural, to the revelation that has been given, and to a God who also can and wants to intervene in a supernatural way showed me that this was a Church that through the ages has not compromised on truth, despite constant attacks.

The Western world is strongly influenced by a secular rationalism that through its worldly attitude refuses to accept God's supernatural intervention. This rationalistic attitude, often presented as scientific fact, has even had a strong influence on modern theology, not least of all Protestant theology. Therefore, the question of miracles became a theologically fundamental question for me, touching the center of our faith. Historicity affects both Christology and ecclesiology.

~

It was fascinating to read about Lourdes, particularly because what happened there took place in a France that had been awash with rationalistic denial ever since the period of the Enlightenment and the French Revolution. In that environment—with its blind faith that everything could be explained by science and that religion, with its so-called superstitious faith in miracles, was irrelevant and unnecessary—remarkable things nevertheless happened in Lourdes.

In a sea of skepticism, God lifted up a young, poor girl, Bernadette Soubirous. In the grotto of Massabielle, near the river Gave, which flows through Lourdes, she met a gloriously radiant woman, whom she gradually understood to be the Virgin Mary. Bernadette was given the task, among other things, of digging with her hands in a place in the grotto from which a spring then gushed forth. When people came and prayed at the spring and drank or took its water with them, a torrent of strong and concrete miracles of healing began. This continued year after year.

In the beginning, I had difficulty believing the history of Lourdes, and the thought of Mary having appeared there felt suspect. Still, there was something here from which I could not escape. Jesus was definitely at the center of everything in Lourdes, even if Mary had a very exalted place as the Mother of Jesus. The fact that the miracles here did not happen in a way that was familiar to me provided me with a new insight: that even I had to come to terms with a bit of rationalistic skepticism.

I read many books about Lourdes. One of them was called *Healing Fire of Christ*, by a Catholic priest, Paul Glynn. He describes documented miracles that have happened in Lourdes in France, Fatima in Portugal, and Knock in Ireland. When I read this book, I could at times hardly believe what I was reading! Certainly, the Protestant Pentecostal-charismatic movement to which I belonged spoke much about healing and engaged in intercessory prayer for the sick. But I had seldom heard about and had never seen the kinds of miracles that have happened in Lourdes. It was also interesting to read how careful they are in Lourdes to sift out what cannot be verified and how long the Church waits until a miracle is deemed authentic. There is a praiseworthy thoroughness in the verification process, and there is no rushing. There is no sensational atmosphere around it all but, rather, a humble wonder and gratitude. At the same time, there is a healthy attitude of focusing not only on miracles and signs but on seeking Jesus for who he is, not only for what he can do for us.

When Birgitta and I traveled to Lourdes in October 2007, we were able to stay a week with the Bethlehem Sisters in their monastery, a bit outside the town in the mountains

above the little village of Saint-Pé-de Bigorre. It was an un-
forgettable experience to come to Lourdes. Despite the fact
that Lourdes is full of shops that sell a multitude of religious
odds and ends, and despite the fact that it is filled with people, Lourdes is picturesque and nice and very influenced by
what God has done there.

In the vicinity of the church—and it is large—there is
no commercial activity. Instead, a very tangible, holy respect
rests over the whole place. Thousands of sick people visit
Lourdes practically every day, and each year around six million people come there. Volunteers from around the whole
world so lovingly and willingly serve them. The sick and the
weak are really important to Jesus, and his loving care for
them was clearly seen in Lourdes through all his servants.

In the morning, we saw hundreds of stretchers and wheelchairs with seriously ill people who were present at the Mass
and received intercessory prayers. Everyone was treated with
such respect and love. The lines in front of the grotto and
the spring were long, but everyone stood very reverently
and prayed. There was no stress at all; rather, a great peace
reigned, and prayer flowed through the entire region. It was
truly astonishing. Though I have traveled the world and been
to many healing conferences and meetings, I have never seen
anything quite like this. Lourdes was so spiritually strong. It
was spiritually alive. Everyone had a place, and everyone was
loved by God. The big area around the Massabielle grotto
where the Virgin Mary appeared to Saint Bernadette is situated next to the river Gave, which runs through Lourdes.
There is a beautiful church built on the hill over the grotto.
Actually, it is three sanctuaries on top of each other. It is
serene even when filled with people. And people are everywhere. It was a great grace to be able to walk around there,
to visit the different chapels, to pray in the grotto, to go

singing in the night procession on the grounds with thousands of people, and in all of this experience God's presence in a very clear way.

~

One person who has meant a great deal to me is the Englishman John Henry Newman (1801–1890). His name had come up when I was young and was studying theology, but since then, I had not thought about him. Now his name began to show up again. I read a bit about him during our year in Israel, mostly fragments and quotes, but I became fascinated, and I realized that I had to dig deeper. On one occasion in Singapore, I bought a larger biography of his life, which I read. This led to my reading another biography, and then one more. I could relate to his life in so many ways.

Eventually, I read his famous autobiography, *Apologia Pro Vita Sua*. Newman was a man with immense intellectual aptitude. He had a conversion at the age of fifteen and then lived in a strongly biblical environment. When he began to study at Oxford, he was a low-church evangelical. Influenced by the theology of his time, he was drawn, for a while, in the more theologically liberal direction. He came into contact with the English high church, however, which gave him more firmness and helped him appreciate both sacraments and ministry. It guided him to the early Church through the study of the Church Fathers. He became the leader of the high-church Oxford movement, published a great many writings and tracts, and strongly emphasized the view of holy orders, historicity, catholicity, and opposition to the interference of the State in the Anglican Church's life and teaching. His coming closer to the early Church, however, was marred by anti-Catholicism for quite some time.

Newman eventually discovered that his Anglican *Via Media*, "middle way", was only a work of his own invention. The way he had first advocated—when he thought everything genuinely Catholic already existed in the Anglican Church—did not measure up to the historical reality. This insight caused him eventually, in 1845, to convert to the Catholic Church, despite a strong inner resistance. His question was: Which church is closest, is in union with, follows, and has most faithfully developed the teaching and essence of the early Church? His answer was: the Catholic Church.

That step was enormously controversial in England during his time, and Newman had to pay a great price. He lost his movement, his popularity, and his friends. It did not stop there, however; instead, he devoted himself to his theological studies and his priestly ministry, and in his older years he became a cardinal. His influence became very great, and more than a hundred years after his conversion and seventy years after his death, he shaped the Second Vatican Council (1962–1965) more than any other theologian. John Henry Newman's life journey and struggle spoke very powerfully to me, and I read his *Apologia* a few more times with very great profit.

∼

For me, the words I had written down earlier regarding the Catholic Church—"discover, appreciate, come closer to, unite with"—had been sign posts for me. We wandered now along an unknown path, and we did not know where it would lead us. We made so many important discoveries, found so much that we appreciated, and were led step by step to the Catholic Church. But I kept pushing away this idea of "uniting with" the Church and let it remain in the background. What I had seen and learned did not automatically mean that I would become a Catholic, I thought. Perhaps all that was in order to deepen my faith and so that I might become more generally educated, work better for unity, and relate better to Catholics? Or was it in order to understand their "language" and begin to understand what they actually meant by different things? I had earlier lived with so many misconceptions. This development was important—yes, absolutely necessary! But certainly it was, first of all, to enrich our own congregation, to broaden and deepen Word of Life that we made these discoveries? I felt strongly that Word of Life had a definite call from God toward unity and that this call was not only about an increasing unity between the Faith Movements and the Pentecostal Movement but concerned the whole Body of Christ, even the Catholic Church.

But Newman came to a point in the end where he could no longer remain with his old convictions in the light of his new discoveries. He stood before a definitive choice, a question of truth that he could not escape. Through the reading of Newman, I began slowly to suspect that even I would have to stand before such a choice. But I did not know yet if it were really so. Or perhaps I suspected it in the depths of my heart, but in any case, I pushed it away from me for a little while longer. The thought was terrifying, considering the great consequences.

I could, in fact, not see how it would be possible for me to become a Catholic. I had a long career behind me. Despite all the ups and downs through the years, I was very happy with Word of Life and felt that the Lord had placed me there. There were so many wonderful people in the congregation, and I truly did not want to hurt them. Nor was there any crisis among us that would take me away from them. A lifetime achievement divided into many different areas of ministry lay behind me, but, at the same time, there was so much more that I wanted to do. The missionary work still spurred me on, and the contact with other Christians had much improved and was important. Many old grudges were gone, and I was more often invited to ecumenical circles. Invitations to conferences from all over the world came all the time.

Why could I not just be content with that and continue to strive for a more general unity between Christians at a calmer pace? Why not also enjoy a little more of what had already been achieved? It might be nice, for once, not to have to face a lot of opposition. And what would people say if I took such a drastic step? It would mean beginning all over again, from "scratch". That is not something one does in the blink of an eye, particularly at my age.

At the same time, I could not escape a gnawing restlessness inside of me. That restlessness could be summed up in the words to which my dear wife, Birgitta, kept returning: "But Ulf, what is it that is *true*?" Not what is easiest, simplest, or most practical at the moment. When Birgitta and I now studied, visited places, and met wonderful Catholics, I thought it could be seen as a kind of general spiritual education. But could this interest really only remain at the level of a sophisticated hobby? Could I devote myself to finding out interesting things, only later to fall back to my old ways again without having been influenced in the depths of my being?

Life is not as superficial as that, and the Lord does not lead us in such ways. The journey of discovery had now changed into an inner battle, where it sometimes felt like I was being pulled so powerfully in two directions that I was about to break. If it was true that the Catholic Church was what she asserted herself to be, what right did we have to remain outside of her full communion? This question became ever more urgent. It never came from people, but only from my own inner being and from our own conversations with each other.

I had met Bishop Anders Arborelius in different settings before, during, and after our years in Israel. In September 2006, I invited him to Word of Life for a public panel discussion. It was a wonderful evening. Bishop Anders was wearing the Carmelite habit, and it was surely the first time most of the members in our congregation had seen either a Catholic bishop or religious Brother in person. For nearly an hour we discussed what we Christians have in common, and afterward there came long and heartfelt applause from a well-filled church. There was no doubt that the congregation liked this. I was very open with the congregation about the fact that I considered it to be a part of my personal and our common calling to work for unity. I preached about this on many different occasions, and once, at a parish meeting in January 2007, I asked them if they could willingly permit me to work further on this path of unity. I received a resounding Yes from the congregation. What this Yes would come to mean, certainly none of us understood.

~

In October 2006, the Lutheran priest Bo Brander invited me to come and preach at the Saint Laurentii foundation in Lund, a Lutheran high-church congregation tailored mainly for university staff and students. This brought back memories from my time as chaplain at the university in Uppsala. For the first time since my years as a priest in the Swedish church, I preached at a high mass. Twenty-five years had passed since I had been ordained a priest by Bishop Bertil Gärtner.

As we were now in Lund, Birgitta and I took the opportunity to drive up to the Norraby monastery to meet the well-known and much-loved Carmelite Brother Wilfrid Stinissen. As a deeply spiritual man and gifted writer, his many books were also read by Swedish Protestants. This first meeting with him was the beginning of a wonderful and important friendship that lasted until his death in 2013. The last time we visited him was a few weeks before his death. The conversations with him meant so much to us and covered many areas. Seldom have I met anyone with whom I at once had such a spontaneous and wonderful connection. It was as though we already knew each other. The way in which Brother Wilfrid encouraged me and had insight into and understanding of both Word of Life and my own situation helped me very much. There was no doubt that he directed us forward during these years with his loving wisdom but without any pressure at all. Gently and kindly he just listened to us. Coming from two very different backgrounds and with differing personalities, we still clicked from the first moment. Intuitively he immediately understood us.

The year that he died, I told him where I thought I stood in relation to the Catholic Church. With a smile, he just said: "Yes, I have noticed that you keep coming back to visit." He challenged me to listen carefully to my heart.

~

Another person who became very important to us was Father Raniero Cantalamessa, whom I first met at an ecumenical conference in Sweden in January 2006. When we later had the ecumenical discussions in Rome that I mentioned earlier, I met him there a few times.

During the fall of 2006, we began to arrange annual trips to Rome for different categories of preachers and leaders of the Word of Life network and within the Faith Movement in Scandinavia. The first trip was with the pastors of Word of Life. The idea was to introduce them to Christianity's historical background and our common faith, to see all the important places in Rome, and to hear interesting speakers. Rome is not only the center of the Catholic Church today, it is also the historical ground where thousands of Christians, including the apostles Peter and Paul, suffered martyrdom during the history of the early Church. The Church grew there as a result of the seed of the blood of the martyrs. Regardless of one's Christian affiliation, one ought to know about this history which is common to all Christians.

Usually we would bring around thirty leaders each time we had a tour like this. Father Cantalamessa came and spoke to the groups, and everyone loved him. On a similar study trip two years later, he came and spoke to our leaders gathered mainly from the former USSR. He then quoted the Letter to the Romans 10:9–10 by asking a question like this: "If a person confesses with his lips that Jesus is Lord, and in his heart believes that God raised him from the dead, what is he then?" Everyone answered: "Saved!" Then he asked, "And if a Catholic confesses with his lips that Jesus is Lord, and in his heart believes that God raised him from the dead, what is he then?" "Saved!" everyone shouted instinctively. Cantalamessa smiled broadly and said: "Perhaps, then, one can stop saying Catholics are not real Christians?" The point hit home with a striking effect. Everyone understood what appalling behavior it was to cast suspicion upon other Christian brothers and sisters, and it became a moment of self-examination that was very healthy for these preachers.

During these trips, we preachers discussed the meaning of unity a lot with each other. It became more and more clear to many in our network of churches that the unity for which Jesus prayed in the Gospel of John, chapter 17, naturally included all Christians and not only our own church and some groups near to us. No, the scope of unity was much wider and deeper than that. This broke down the prejudices of many and challenged them to dare to open their closed circles. Unity builds on love and truth and results in a deeper communion. The newly discovered and then deepened communion between Christians is sweet and precious and must be protected.

Such a unity erases hidden agendas and does not allow itself to be enmeshed in predictable patterns. Nor is this unity a kind of conference or working committee, which is intensive for a short period of united activities. The longing for true unity in spirit and in truth causes one to seek farther. One must follow the way of Jesus, sacrifice oneself, and take up one's cross daily. This desire leads to listening to and learning from others. It challenges the heart to open itself, to trust in one's brothers and sisters and put them first, before one's own ambitions. That is certainly difficult. If the unity about which Jesus speaks and for which he prays is to be a unity built on truth, it needs to be both self-searching and reconciling. It makes amends for injustices and prays for the wounds and divisions in the Body of Christ. The Lord wants to heal us when he heals and unites his Body. And this desire for unity results, in the end, in a visible unity.

There are three classical images that describe unity in a clear way. One of these images alone is not enough to comprehend the fullness of God's intention with respect to Church unity.

The first image is *the People of God* and the fellowship between the different members of this people. It can be a unity in diversity. God is in the midst of his people and is a loving Father who takes care of all his children.

The image of the Church as *the Body of Christ* is the second image. It speaks of how dependent we are on each other because of the fact that life is communicated through the different members. This image also reminds us of the order that must exist in a body, where the different organs have their own special place and function in order for life to continue and health to be maintained. Jesus Christ is truly present through all his members in his Body.

The image of *God's Temple* is the third image, and it speaks of a precise, careful, external order as well as of a clearly constructed structure. A temple is not a spontaneous, slipshod work. In a living temple, there is a strong, inner, holy, spiritual life—our spiritual temple worship. Both the external and the internal are necessary together, so that the function of the temple—to sacrifice to and praise God—will be authentic and pleasing to God. This temple building is an external, structured, visible unity. The different cut stones are carefully placed in a harmonious way where they are meant to be, to the greater glory of God. The outward, visible structure of the Temple shelters and protects God's tangible and real presence among his people, the *shekinah*, the glory of God inside the Temple, in the Holy of Holies. The visible structure and the invisible Glory are two necessary components of the Temple.

Through these three images we can see that the Triune God is tangibly present in his Church and also united with his people whom he wills should be one.

I think that we make it too easy for ourselves if we are content only with a kind of unity that is a generally open attitude of fellowship toward other Christians. If that is the case, we can just be generous and let everyone remain different. But if we do not dare to go farther and prayerfully and lovingly reflect on what it is that actually separates us and why, we miss out on much. We must dare to question our positions and prayerfully consider how to go forward until we reach full unity.

There is no doubt that the goal must be an external, visible unity filled with an inner and strong spiritual life. When the Church was born, she was one in mind and spirit. This unity could be seen from the outside, despite her weaknesses, failures, and trials. I hope that she will once again be like that before Jesus Christ returns. But the way there is not easy. It will mean testing, temptation, pain, and deep conversion. Just like Mary, we will come to experience how a sword pierces our souls. We must humble ourselves before one another and before God in order for the truth really to be revealed and make us all free—free to be deeply united with those to whom we belong and to whom we are called to love.

It was when I started to realize this that the question became urgent. Not the least because it became so clear to me how wrong it was of us Protestants to try to create a self-chosen form of unity that kept the Catholic Church on the outside. Many do this out of fear. If you want to be theologically serious, consistent, and truthful, this is impossible and dishonest. If lasting unity is to be attained, the Catholic Church must be brought into the equation. And then the claims of the Catholic Church must also be considered.

I was now in a place where everything was coming to a head: Was the Catholic Church what she made herself out to be? And if that was the case, what consequences did this have for all of us?

Chapter 8

Birgitta: A Growing Desire to Share Our Experiences

When I look through my notes from that period now, ten years after our return home from Israel to Sweden, I notice a lot of things. I see traces of our longing for "the historical churches", but I also see intensive, joy-filled work with Word of Life. Periodically, the work was very demanding.

But we were not downcast. No, there was so much that spurred us on and gave us joy. At the Word of Life Europe Conference in the summer of 2005, we had ecumenical guests—the Evangelical Sisters of Mary from Darmstadt were there as well as Catholic priests from the Koinonia movement in Italy. Large groups of young people from Poland, both Catholics and Protestants, had now begun to attend. We rejoiced over all these new friends and believed that the Lord wanted to renew and deepen Word of Life.

An experience in October has become a precious memory. Together with some Italian Catholic friends, we visited Subiaco, not far from Rome. There Saint Benedict, the founder of Western monasticism, lived for some years in a cave during the late fifth century. We walked up the steep path to this cave, and we fell on our knees together and prayed for the unity of the Church and for a re-evangelization of Europe. These Catholics, who had such a charismatic spirituality, made us realize, time and time again, how little most Protestants in the Nordic countries knew about what the Catholic Church is and does. This Church is constantly working hard to save souls, to strengthen believers in their faith, to stand up against the secularization of our societies—and we did not know about it! It is embarrassing to be confronted with one's prejudices—but so refreshing to abandon them.

~

A question we often discussed in the board meetings of Word of Life was: "Where is Word of Life going?" Yes, already in 2006 questions were in the air, and we were being observed and judged by people who were making guesses about our interest in the Catholic Church. Naturally, some wrong conclusions were made. There was even speculation on the Internet, in all seriousness, that Ulf was secretly working together with Pope Benedict XVI and was about to affiliate the Word of Life church as a body into the Catholic Church.

We had, however, no such scheming plans, though we were definitely working to bring down walls, increase knowledge, and warm up frozen relationships between ourselves and other churches in Sweden.

We continued to read books, and that spring we read Scott Hahn's excellent book about Mary: *Hail, Holy Queen: The Mother of God in the Word of God*. It answered many of my questions and deepened my understanding of the role of the Virgin Mary.

Besides the work in the congregation, Ulf was always writing. I began to write a series of illustrated books for children, where I told about my experiences and adventures as a missionary child in India. I also wrote a little mini-book about the vocation of being a mother and how contemporary Swedish society makes it hard for those who would like to be stay-at-home-mothers when their children are small.

~

On Pentecost of 2006, Pope Benedict gathered all the charismatic movements in a large meeting at Saint Peter's Square. Our friend Kim had secured seats for the three of us on the huge platform reserved primarily for bishops and cardinals but with seats also for other guests. We had a great view of both the pope and the 350,000 joyful people who filled the square and surrounding streets. Obviously we had learned a little bit about the Catholic faith in the past years, but this charismatic explosion of song and joy struck us with amazement! People had traveled there from all corners of the world, and their flags fluttered in the wind. Different groups sang joyful charismatic songs, and the pope spoke in his gentle and warm manner to the people. I must confess that we felt like we were dreaming, for we had never imagined that a meeting with the pope could be such a joyful and informal event!

After Pentecost, we traveled on to Fiuggi, where we were invited to be present at a conference organized by ICCRS (International Catholic Charismatic Renewal Services). Since 1967 the Catholic charismatic renewal had swept over the whole world, and now we understood that it is still very much alive in the Catholic Church. We heard that the Catholic charismatic movement existed in about 230 countries around the world and had about 160 million members. Well, what can you say about that when you come from taciturn Scandinavia where we Christians often can feel rather small, struggling to serve the Lord in our very secular societies. It was refreshing and wonderful to hear about this great Church and even to hear that all the popes since the charismatic renewal first began in the 1960s have blessed this movement.

In Fiuggi, we met Patti Mansfield and Kevin Ranaghan, two of those who first experienced the baptism of the Spirit within the Catholic Church. It was in February 1967 that some teachers and students at Duquesne University in the United States experienced this special outpouring of the Spirit. Some of them had read *The Cross and the Switchblade*, by David Wilkerson, and began to long for the experience of the Spirit that was described in this book. From this university, the renewal spread farther to Notre Dame University in South Bend, and then on and on.

We introduced ourselves to Patti as a Protestant pastor and his wife and told her how we now felt called to acquaint ourselves more with the Catholic faith, which was viewed with so much skepticism in our Protestant context. It was very interesting to talk to Patti and hear about the charismatic renewal in the Catholic Church from this experienced and lovely person. I also remember especially a dynamic Maltese bishop from Australia, Bishop Joe Grech. Just watching him celebrate the Mass and worshipping the Lord together with the other priests and bishops, with hands lifted in praise, was so special to Ulf and me. In my diary, I have summed up everything with one word: Astounding!

～

As usual, we led a large trip to Israel in June with participants from many countries. Ulf and I had now gone through a great change of attitude. In the past, we had a complicated relationship with the Catholic and Orthodox church buildings in many important places in Israel. To our Scandinavian Protestant taste, they were too cluttered with unfamiliar objects. So we always opted for the simpler churches by the lake of Galilee and the beautiful church of Saint Anna by the Pool of Bethesda in Jerusalem. For many years, we avoided the church of the Holy Sepulchre. We were simply not able to bring ourselves to see beyond the walls darkened by time and incense and all the oriental expressions of piety, so different from our own tradition. We just could not manage the stillness and the traditional expressions of the Christian faith. We called this "rigid" and "religious". It is sad that we were so narrow and did not understand better.

After our years in Israel, this completely changed. Now we took the pilgrims to all the fantastic churches with joy, and we had also included the monastery in Beit Jimal in our program.

We wondered at first how this would work with all our free-church people from Scandinavia and the Russians, Chinese, and Indians. But we worried unnecessarily! Our secretary, Avigail, was now a postulant in the monastery, and for every busload of pilgrims that came, she told in her radiant way about how she had been a part of Word of Life, had worked for us, and then had received the vocation to enter the monastery! She told them about the life of prayer the Sisters lived and explained that they compared their mission to the heart in a body. Through their prayers, blessings are pumped out into the Church and the world, she explained. Our travelers understood this language. When the bus filled up again for further adventures, we saw that many eyes had welled up with tears. Very many said at the end that the visit to the monastery was the most beautiful moment of the whole trip! We were so happy to be able to bring down a few walls between believers!

Before we left Israel, we had the great joy of being present when Avigail made her first profession of vows and was clothed in her white habit. We sat up in the choir loft with her Messianic Jewish friends, our Arabic Christian friends, and even a few friends from Word of Life. The whole service was in French, but I still remembered some of the French I had learned in school and could understand a great deal. It was so beautiful to see Avigail make her vows on her knees before Sister Isabelle. We had never seen anything like it. Avigail received her new name at this time, Sister Avigail-Marie, and she then went around to all the Sisters to receive their loving welcome.

~

That fall we organized a study trip to Rome for the first time. We stayed in the Birgitta-House at Piazza Farnese, which provided the opportunity to recall all that I had read about Saint Birgitta's life in Rome and how strongly she had influenced the age in which she lived. Every morning we walked off to the Centro Pro Unione near Piazza Navona. In the hall where we had our discussions and lectures, Vivaldi's *Four Seasons* had once been played for the first time in Rome.

One of the speakers was Lord David Alton from England, a British Catholic politician who is strongly engaged in ethical questions and in the suffering and persecuted Church. Jim Puglisi, Director of the Centro Pro Unione and a Franciscan Brother and professor, challenged us to think more deeply. We also heard from a priest from Rome, Father Alberto Pacini, from the church of Saint Anastasia, who reaches out to the marginalized and to drug addicts. Father Alberto had also started a movement of Perpetual Adoration in his church. He explained to our Protestant colleagues that this means that there is always someone, day and night, praying in a side chapel before the Most Blessed Sacrament. Teresa Rossi, a young woman and a doctor of theology, won the hearts of many. Her combination of a warm personality and a gift for teaching was impressive. And, of course, Charles Whitehead spoke, and who can resist the charm of an English gentleman? He has enormous experience in spreading understanding of the charismatic renewal and has worked a great deal with ecumenical questions. Finally, we had the honor of hearing Father Raniero Cantalamessa, who is preacher to the papal household—in other words, the pope's special preacher. This humble servant of the Lord went straight to everyone's hearts.

We visited many beautiful churches, the Forum Romanum, the Arch of Titus, the Catacombs, and much more. What moved the pastors in a powerful way was the Scavi, the excavations under Saint Peter's Basilica. There, you can walk in passageways from the first century and see how the Romans buried their dead. Finally, you reach the grave of the apostle Peter. In previous chapters, we have told about our own powerful experience when we came there for the first time. And now it was so stunning to see the Holy Spirit touch the pastors as they stood in front of this great apostle, whom they all admired so much.

We really felt we had found a method in these study trips that worked very well. We had fun together, and in the evenings and at coffee breaks we had lively discussions about everything we had experienced and heard. So, we continued these trips to Rome to promote general knowledge and spiritual edification for many years with different groups from the Word of Life network.

～

At that time, our youngest son, Benjamin, was studying at Wheaton College in Chicago. The first time we went there to visit him we needed a GPS in the rental car to be sure to find our way from the airport. We typed in the address of his college, which was located in the suburbs. But after a while, we began to wonder if something was wrong, because we were led deeper and deeper into Chicago. But we obeyed the voice from the GPS—until it said: "You have reached your destination." We looked out and did indeed see a university—but the sign read: Loyola University. A Jesuit university! We laughed and wondered how in the world that could have happened. So the Jesuits were our destination. We did not know that! Well, we eventually found Wheaton College, of course, and had a few nice days with Benjamin, and we also accompanied him to the Orthodox church he usually attended.

During a student exchange program in the spring of 2006, Benjamin had visited the Franciscan University of Steubenville with a group of students at Wheaton. There, he got a chance to chat with Scott Hahn, who was teaching at the university. Their discussion had lasted for hours, and they had had a great exchange of ideas, which led Scott Hahn to email us and tell us about it. We were, of course, surprised to receive an unexpected email from the well-known author. By that time, we had read many of his books.

At the end of 2006, we flew over to the United States again for a leadership meeting at Oral Roberts University in Tulsa, Oklahoma, and then we also took the opportunity to visit Scott and Kimberly Hahn together with Benjamin. We had very good discussions and accompanied their large family to Mass in their church. In their home, Scott took us down to his huge library in the basement, and Ulf was naturally thrilled. He could have stayed there for several days. What a treasure trove!

To have this direct contact with Scott and Kimberly felt like a gift from God. Since they both came from Evangelical Protestant backgrounds but had by then been Catholics for many years, we could understand each other well. They had become Catholics at a younger age, when Scott was on the way to becoming a pastor. There were both similarities and differences between their encounter and ours with the Catholic Church.

Back in Sweden, we started a study group in our home. Many had questions about Catholicism, and rumors about us were still flourishing on the Internet. That is why we thought it would be good if together, with a group of our younger leaders in the congregation, we could discuss and study a few questions. We had different books as a foundation. Among them was Ulf's own book, *Spiritual Roots* (*Andliga rötter*) and Peter Kreeft's books *Back to Virtue* and *Catholic Christianity*. We continued with these gatherings for several years, and it was greatly appreciated and surely did much good. Many feared "the Catholic influence" on Word of Life. But it is impossible to answer the apprehensive questions of people if they do not want to learn what the Church has always believed throughout history. Naturally, the members of Word of Life have a strong, devoted faith in God. I do not think I need to try to record all the central Christian truths that are embraced there with burning hearts; the love for Jesus Christ and the eagerness for mission are clearly manifest. It is when things and expressions seem foreign that the worrying starts. Different denominations have different vocabularies, and that at times creates misunderstanding between us. But then there are the questions that definitely meet with direct opposition: Mary, purgatory, the pope. Even the priestly ministry and the doctrine of transubstantiation can trouble many.

Ulf felt that he did not want to force his own thoughts

and inquiries regarding these questions on our congregation. Little by little, he gave instructions on things of which he had become convinced. He wrote articles and books, and those who wanted to could follow along in this.

In March 2007, we traveled to Rome, invited to participate in a group that led informal ecumenical dialogues between nondenominational charismatic Christians and the Catholic Church. The dialogues had been going on for a couple of years. It was a rather large group of people and included some from new charismatic churches in the United States, England, and Germany and, from the Catholic side, some people from the charismatic renewal and even select Catholic theologians. The discussion days were listed as a "Gathering in the Holy Spirit." The idea was to bring up important questions, such as the view of mission, suffering, and our respective identities, and in such a way we could come to understand the outlook of one another.

Ulf wrote up the papers for the nondenominationals. It was a demanding responsibility, but also a good opportunity for him to delve deeper into the subject in this way. For me, it was nice to do the proofreading. Many years later, these essays were translated into Swedish and became a part of Ulf's book *Ancient Paths* (*Urgamla stigar*).

~

Charles Whitehead invited us to come to Ilfracombe in England in April 2007. As we have mentioned, Charles' wife, Sue, is Anglican, and as such they live out their vocation to Christian unity in their own family. In the little picturesque coastal town of Ilfracombe, they have created a spiritual oasis for charismatic Catholics and Protestants. People have told us that their conference *Celebrate* has strengthened and saved the spiritual lives of many people. Swarms of children and youth are also present.

Ulf also gave a talk there, and when we went home, we felt refreshed from having met so many wonderful people. In particular, we remember Bishop Joe Grech from Australia as a radiant, warm person. We were sad when we heard a few years later that he had died of a blood disease. Rest in peace, Bishop Grech!

In the late spring of 2007, Ulf was invited by the Oasis movement, a revival movement in the Swedish church, to a conference in Gothenburg. It was particularly nice for Ulf to be able to preach at Liseberg, the amusement park in his hometown. In the same building where he preached, he had been a part of a pop band competition as a teenager. He jokingly said that to be able to preach there now could almost be seen as suitable reparation for old sins!

Among the friends at Oasis, we were met with warm love and appreciation. Many Lutheran priests contacted Ulf during those days, and it was interesting to see that, for them, Ulf was still a priest. I heard the expression *character indelebilis* mentioned, which alludes to the indelible mark or character that one receives in priestly ordination. This is something God gives. It was beautiful and moving to witness this bond that seemed to be present between Ulf and many priests in the Swedish church.

The relationship between Word of Life and the Pentecostal movement in Sweden has not always been the best through the years. We have had a very good fellowship with many individuals, but with the movement itself, there was often friction. They felt that we were too self-assured, and they took a skeptical position toward our instruction of the faith. And we thought that they only disliked the fact that a new revivalist movement was influencing the Swedish free churches. In any case, reconciliation between our groups was needed, particularly during this time when we were focused on unity. Then, out of the blue we received an invitation from the Pentecostal Pastor Jack-Tommy Ardenfors, a leading pastor in the Swedish Pentecostal movement. Even as far back as the 1980s, there had been a real clash between Ulf and him. Now, about twenty years later, they were reconciled and preached together at the Swedish Pentecostal's summer conference. It was clear that many Pentecostals also longed for greater unity and peace between our movements. It was really wonderful to share their fellowship, and I see it as a work of God when such wounds are healed. The following year, Ulf was again invited to preach there.

In the summer, when we did our usual tour to Israel, we also had time to visit the monastery in Beit Jimal. This time, we were surprised to see that Sister Isabelle, who is the Superior of the whole Order, had gathered all twenty-five prioresses from around the world. We came only to visit, but Sister Isabelle took advantage of the opportunity to ask us to tell about "our journey" to these Sisters. I was quite nervous as I wondered what I was going to say. We sat outside in a large circle. We told how God had led us to realize how we had been judgmental toward the Catholic Church and had been converted from that attitude. I told how, for myself, it began with Saint Birgitta, which later led to Mary. The Sisters were happy and amazed that a Protestant pastor and his wife could speak in this way, and for us it was quite an experience to meet all these nuns.

That fall the relationship to our high-church friends in the Swedish Lutheran Church led to Ulf being asked to give a lecture at their annual meeting. We were happily surprised by the warm response Ulf received. It felt like springtime for ecumenism. Perhaps the winter was over, and more normal relations could develop, both with the Swedish church and with the free-churches?

~

In our study of Mary, we had tried to understand the Marian apparitions about which we had heard. This idea that Mary had appeared in certain places was difficult to accept in the beginning. But I have already told how I struggled with the questions about Mary in Jerusalem and reached a point where I could understand and assent to her unique and wonderful role in heaven and in the Body of Christ.

The Europe Conference at Word of Life, with its ten thousand participants, means a demanding week of work. After the conference in the summer of 2007, we traveled to Ireland for a vacation, driving through the country by car with our friends and fellow Word of Life pastors, Joakim and Maria Lundqvist. It was a fantastic week, during which we saw beautiful places and read about Saint Patrick, the great hero of the faith from the fifth century in Ireland. As a Word of Life member, one never speaks about saints, but one speaks quite frequently about heroes of the faith. These heroes of the faith are often great Protestant missionaries and pioneers, but certain Catholic saints can occasionally slip into the category of heroes of the faith. In any case, we followed in the footsteps of Saint Patrick and saw places where he had worked. We were all deeply fascinated by how he challenged paganism and Christianized Ireland.

We had heard about the little village of Knock, which has a fascinating history from the nineteenth century. Here, several villagers received a supernatural vision near the church in the village. They saw Joseph and Mary together with John the Evangelist and, next to them, an altar on which a lamb stood. Angels were hovering over them all. The news of this apparition spread, and people came streaming to this place. After this, many have related that healings and conversions took place there.

The apparition is now beautifully represented in white marble, exactly where it took place that rainy evening in 1879. What impressed us there was the stillness, the order, the beauty, and how pilgrims seeking spiritual help are continually welcomed.

Yes, these sites where apparitions took place are undeniably captivating and bewildering, and one can surely give them too great a place in one's spiritual life. We have understood that there are problems with some who develop a fixation with respect to certain revelations. But even on the Protestant side, there are very similar human peculiarities. At this point, we ourselves were only at the research stage. The Catholic world is so gigantic, and there were always things we wanted to investigate or read more about.

So our Marian research journey in October 2007 took us to Lourdes, in the south of France. When I told my ninety-two-year-old Methodist mother that we were thinking of going there for a few days to rest, she smiled with interest and said: "Oh, the place of the little girl and the grotto." I was happy that she knew about the event there and did not show any concern about our traveling there.

We had read about it beforehand and looked forward to seeing this special place where Mary revealed an important truth about herself in 1858. As Ulf mentioned, it was a poor little girl, Bernadette, who saw Mary one day when she was gathering wood by the riverbed. What she saw was a radiant young girl in a white dress with a blue sash around her waist. The vision of Mary, which spoke of penance and prayer for the conversion of sinners, was repeated many times in slightly different ways. Bernadette did not want to be deceived by any false vision and prayed earnestly to God for protection. She was disbelieved and ridiculed by the whole district, but she could not deny what she had seen and heard. What is special about this vision was that Mary—when asked who she was—answered: "I am the Immaculate Conception." Those were words that the little girl did not understand, but she repeated them to herself until she came to the parish priest, who was very astonished, indeed, truly shocked. This convinced him in the end that the vision was authentic. It is a beautiful story, and Ulf and I were taken by the peace and beauty in this place.

~

In our church in Uppsala we had been lacking an altar, and at communion services we had to arrange a temporary altar. We now felt that this was not good enough. The members of Word of Life come from different backgrounds, free churches, the Pentecostal movement, the Lutheran Church and also straight from "the world". So, some thought it was a "Catholic idea" to have an altar, despite the fact that there are altars in every little Lutheran church throughout the whole country. Now there was a longing among many, though, to have our church hall look a little more like a church and not a plain conference hall. So, on Christmas night 2008, we dedicated a beautiful altar table made of ash wood and designed by an architect friend. Everyone was happy. Not the least myself. Earlier that year we had also finally erected a large cross on the roof of our church building. These two things—the cross and the altar—led to heated discussions on the Internet and around many kitchen tables!

~

That fall I turned sixty years old, and our whole family celebrated it with a wonderful weekend in Rome. I have a dear memory of the church of San Clemente, where one of our grandchildren stood rooted to the spot in front of a large crucifix on a side wall. Jesus' body looked very realistic, and our little grandson wondered if it might be the real Jesus hanging there. He knew, of course, that Jesus is risen and in heaven, but still . . . This looked so very real.

In the Church of the Jesuits, Il Gesu, another grandchild asked his mother what that box was by the church wall, and she explained that there one could confess one's sins to a priest and receive forgiveness. He immediately went down on his knees, and his mother asked what he wanted to confess. A sweet little conversation followed about the necessity not to get angry with his siblings but, rather, to forgive them when it was necessary.

In November, we had another study trip to Rome, this time with the leading pastors of Word of Life's centers in Moscow, Siberia, the Ukraine, Armenia, Uzbekistan, and Azerbaijan. These are such good and amazing people, and they are leaders of great churches in their respective countries. Some of them have churches with thousands of members. So not all of them were inclined to befriend the Catholic Church. But eventually these days in Rome nevertheless meant much to them, and their understanding of the worldwide Catholic Church and our common history grew.

More and more people were discussing us on Facebook and other social media. When there are converts from the Catholic Church in the Protestant churches, it is often more difficult and the emotional reactions can be strong. Ulf tried his best to reassure these friends that we did not have any hidden agenda and that we were not trying to impose anything on them that they did not want to be a part of.

⁓

For me personally, my time was filled more and more with the care of my elderly parents, who were both ninety-four years old. That winter, they had finally felt that, for my father's sake, it was necessary for them to move to a nursing home. We siblings did all we could to help them and keep them company.

My beloved father died in August 2009. He had been faithful to the Methodist Church his whole life and had encouraged Ulf to continue with ecumenism, even with Catholics. His ecumenical mentality could not tolerate being negative toward any church. He showed only joy and encouraged Ulf to continue on the path we were now on.

⁓

We knew that we ourselves had begun to follow a path that must lead to some form of change, but how, when, and where—this we did not know. The responsibility for Word of Life lay upon our shoulders, and it was a question not just of Uppsala, but of our whole network of around two hundred thousand people in different countries. We prayed fervently to the Lord for help to understand his will. Saint Birgitta's prayer became ours: *"Show me the way and make me willing to follow it."*

Chapter 9

Ulf: What About the Church and the Pope?

After our return to Sweden, my responsibility for Word of Life had not lessened but, rather, increased and become more multifaceted. At the same time, a desire in me deepened to understand the Catholic faith better. This hardly passed unnoticed, and criticism was not long in coming. It came not only from the outside, that is, from Christians in Sweden and other countries, but also from the inside, from members within our own congregation. Those who were critical reacted to my sudden change from a more negative attitude toward the Catholic Church to a clearly greater openness. Far from everyone was critical, however.

It was important for me to explain my present point of view and why I had changed my way of thinking. But at this time I was not at the point of converting. And certainly I disputed the claim that I was secretly trying to convert Word of Life.

Sometimes the accusations could be simply absurd. With certain critics, their knowledge of the Catholic Church was minimal. Even fundamental and generally accepted Christian ideas could suddenly be called "Catholicism" and be dismissed without any other reason. It was as though an allergy had broken out in Scandinavia against the Catholic Church. In order not to become defensive, I had continually to remind myself of how little knowledge I myself had had about the Catholic faith before. I was well aware of things I had thought and said.

This had ultimately become a question of truth for me, and the truth can never harm us, only free us. I now could see that we in our Protestant circles did not have the right information about the Catholic faith. On the contrary. It was colored by centuries of theological and political disputes and modern rivalry about winning souls in different mission fields. In the Pentecostal-charismatic milieu, this was a sensitive topic. I also began to realize that a part of the free-church identity is built upon being *against* something else. It is therefore lived as a theological and psychological reaction against what has happened in the past. A theology built on reactions is, in the long term, never sound.

The fact that I was studying the Catholic Church with such interest did not mean that I was about to go "from one extreme to the other", as someone later claimed in a newspaper article. No, it meant that I was coming closer to something that was much broader and higher, the actual heart and center of the Christian faith in its classic formulation.

I had to come to terms with the lack of historicity and also the elitism that comes from thinking that what is latest is the best. C.S. Lewis so aptly calls this "chronological snobbery". In the free churches and among many in my own movement, the lack of knowledge and interest in the history of Christianity often results in pride and a strange and negative view of the Catholic Church. A genuine revival movement takes worldliness and unbelief to task among the people of God and points out the need for conversion as the road to a living relationship with God. However, Church history is seen as a development where the "revival movements" are considered to be the only real expression of true spiritual life. This is often joined to the belief that only these movements go back to the true, "original New Testament" Church.

It is certainly true that in every generation, the Church needs renewal—revival movements are indispensable—but attitudes that are too negative toward the history of the Church lead astray. Something is missing in the view that such movements have of the Church, something that would anchor them in history and create a sound continuity. It was this insight that was growing in me.

~

These thoughts led me to begin studying ecclesiology, the theological study of the Church, more seriously. It was in ecclesiology that both the problem and the solution could be found. The problem lay in the idea of what a true and genuine unity in the Body of Christ actually is. Is the historical development of Christianity, with its divisions in Protestantism that constantly give birth to new movements and denominations, really a work of the Holy Spirit? Or is it instead sometimes the result of the inability or unwillingness of people to live together? Is the Protestant view of unity as something that already exists, though invisibly, sufficient? Is it enough that we have some foundational things in common but that each movement works in its own way?

In the tense relationship that exists between different Christian denominations, it can easily happen that every division is legitimized and considered something natural, a work of the Spirit in every generation. If you add to that a view of the Church that speaks in terms of a constant need for new developments, you come close to legitimizing every event as "renewal".

I began to realize that this did not measure up theologically. God does not want his people to be divided. He does not want his house to be torn down. He does not want the Body of Christ to be broken. A branch that is cut off from the tree trunk can look as though it is alive for awhile, but it soon withers. A limb that is cut off from the body can no longer function; it inevitably dies. People who fight among themselves and are divided do not survive; they destroy each other. Division brings about weakness. The central meaning of unity in the Bible stood out ever more clearly for me. Unity comes from the love of God that draws us together into the deep communion of the Trinity. Division lies in the essence of sin itself and separates us from one another and from God.

When I seriously drew closer to the Catholic Church, the result was a definitive reevaluation of ecclesiology. It was precisely the Church, the Body of Christ, that began to fascinate me, and I began to see her incredible meaning. When I heard Catholic theologians and preachers like Raniero Cantalamessa speak about how passionate love for Christ also meant a passionate love for his Church, it struck a deep chord within me. I realized how underdeveloped my Church view actually was and what a poor understanding I had of the Church—and thus of the love for Jesus in his Body, the Church.

Up to now, my view of the Church had emphasized the fact that we are an assembly of Christians who love God and *do* things together. It was clearly activist-oriented. We had certainly spoken warmly about the Body of Christ and its unity, but unity was still so invisible within the Protestant church. It was Jesus, not the church, that was important, we thought. The church stood mostly for what was troublesome, the holy rubbish that stood in the way of an establishment of God's Kingdom today.

To change my perspective now—from the excessively individualistic Protestant view and from the free-church overemphasis on the autonomous local congregation—meant a great liberation for me. I realized that in this way of thinking there might very well exist not only an "evangelical freedom" but also a bit of selfishness, individually and collectively. Behind the talk of "freedom", there could be a drive for the false autonomy of our ego, where one simply does not want to conform to anything at all. I realized that this was also a path that constantly led to new divisions and to an ever-greater fragmentation of the Body of Christ.

The church began to appear to me now as *one* single Church. She is *one* body—a visible body. She is *one* holy people. She is universal and common to all, and, yes, she is catholic. She is far-reaching and yet welded together, both organically and organizationally. She is apostolic, in direct relation to the apostles, both to their teaching and their office.

I now saw the Church as something holy and majestic, organic and structured, free and alive, so steady that she could not be shaken. She is ever present and ever continuous, sacramental and charismatic, present on earth and active in heaven. She is, and remains, all of this simultaneously in her journey through time. This was the Catholic breadth, length, height, and depth, and all of this fascinated and intrigued me deeply.

My joy was not obscured by the fact that the Church had often toiled in our world in great lowliness, disgrace, opposition, and weakness and was sometimes marred with scandals, confusion, and worldliness, since we, the members, are sinners. We are God's children, but we sin, and we have not

reached perfection. We strive for holiness, but we have not
yet arrived.

When a pastor friend asked me, after I had been received
into the Catholic Church, what it was I had seen that he
had not seen, I could only answer with two words: "The
Church!" I had discovered how Jesus is one with and so tangibly present in his Church. The Church is not a problem
that prevents us from seeing Jesus but, rather, the unique and
singular means through which Jesus lets himself be seen and
manifested in the world today. He reveals himself through
his Body, his people, and his temple. I had discovered Jesus
in his Church more than ever before.

But the subject of ecclesiology was more sensitive than
I had first understood. To have different viewpoints here
sometimes was perceived as criticizing someone's beloved
family member. I think it is important to say that when I
began to make these discoveries there was never in my mind
the idea that Protestants were not real Christians. I do not
think that way and have never thought that way. I was just
so happy to realize that through the Church we share in
the fullness, in the whole truth, and in that which is truly
authentic. What is genuine and true will last. It will, in
the long term, have a unifying and restoring effect on all
of us.

∼

This process had started when I was looking for a means to
remedy what was lacking in our church-planting endeavors.
But when I examined our spiritual life, our dogmatic foundation, and our view of what a church really is, it became
all the more clear that it was not enough to make minor
corrections. We were part of a much deeper disunion than

what I had first understood, and it became ever more difficult merely to take a pragmatic position. Again and again, I was challenged by the question of what the essence of the Church actually is. The question of truth became more and more pressing. Where was the most legitimate expression of Christ's Church on earth? What position should I take in regard to this?

Many times, I discussed these questions with my friends and colleagues but also even with pastors in other movements, and it was often here that things got heated. The source of irritation obviously lay in the perception of the exclusive claims of the Catholic Church. I had now begun to see things differently. Maybe the Catholics were, in fact, right in their understanding of the Church? In that case, they were right in maintaining their own distinctive character, since it entailed being faithful to the Gospel and faithful to Jesus as Lord over the Church.

If this is the case, then the Church deserves great appreciation. She is no obstacle that one must go around or overcome if one wants to get something done, as some of her critics would claim. The Body of Christ with the Real Presence of Jesus is God's gift, God's means of salvation and ultimate sacrament to the world. The Church cannot simply be something spontaneous or pragmatic, something arbitrarily thrown together. However—and this is important—the Church can develop through the ages.

~

There is a common false notion among free-church members that everything to do with the Church and the Christian life must be expressly written in the Bible, and only there, in order to be valid. On this point, I was now challenged.

And here John Henry Newman came to my help. His theology, that the original revelation with its biblical foundation is like a seed that later develops and grows through the history of the Church, is both biblically based and reasonable. Everything that is Christian and true does not need to be explicitly written in the Bible, but it must be in accord with the Bible and never contradict it.

This means, for example, that the ministry of bishops, the episcopate, which was founded in the New Testament, could develop in order to meet the needs of coming generations. Revelation as such is finished and complete. The Church has the mission in every generation to transmit and interpret it. In that way, the Church can serve all people, in all ages, and at the same time be faithful to the original Church. Such a development must follow the original, in the same way that from an acorn always comes an oak tree and not, say, an alligator. The development of the Church and the development of dogma can never mean a change of nature or character but must remain faithful to the original revelation.

I now had a greater understanding of what an authentic teaching office actually entails. As priests in the universal priesthood, which is mentioned in 1 Peter 2:5–8, we all have access to God's Word and should read the Scriptures daily for our edification. But we are not left completely on our own in order to understand everything and should definitely not build a body of doctrine by ourselves, either. The Church has within herself, by the great Providence and working of the Spirit, a teaching office that has the authorization and anointing of the Spirit to keep guard over the doctrine and deepen the understanding of that which has been given once and for all.

Compare this to a game of soccer. There are players—the

Christians. There is a rule book—biblical revelation. And there are referees—the teaching office (Magisterium). The referee is there, not to prevent us from playing, but rather to help us play according to the rules. If we interpret all the rules in our own way, there is the inevitable risk that we will change what does not suit us and read the rules selectively. We will pay attention to what suits us and leave out the rest.

When it is said that we do not need any overarching teaching office, since we ourselves have the Holy Spirit within us —I hear this constantly in certain circles—it is a misunderstanding of the Bible's fundamental principle of the Incarnation, of the idea of the sacramental. Jesus Christ has given us a teaching office in the Church (Eph 4:11–13), which is the physical, visible aspect of the Spirit's revelatory and teaching function (Jn 14:26). Jesus gave us the apostles and their instruction—the apostolic teaching—which should be preserved and followed throughout the whole history of the Church until Jesus returns (Acts 2:42, Jude v. 3). The teaching ministry is not there to suppress us and prevent us from thinking for ourselves; rather, it is anointed by the Spirit in order to help us find the right way. This teaching ministry exists embodied in the bishops, the successors of the apostles.

So many pieces fell into place when I realized this. I understood that the Reformation idea of "Scripture alone", (*sola Scriptura*) however good the intention may have been, simply was not biblical. This teaching is not mentioned in the Bible or in the history of the Church before the sixteenth century. By its openness to arbitrary interpretations, this teaching has led to a multitude of different, individual, separate understandings and doctrinal divisions.

The fact that one dismisses "Scripture alone" does not mean that one denies the authority of the Bible. The Bible is and remains the Holy Scripture, God's eternal Word, inspired by the Holy Spirit. "All Scripture is inspired by God and profitable for teaching, for reproof, for correction, and for training in righteousness, that the man of God may be complete, equipped for every good work" (2 Tim 3:16–17).

We live by the Scriptures, but we also need the teaching office that helps us to understand the Bible, so that we will be able to live out the fullness of our faith in the Church. There is a living teaching office in the Church through the bishops, which is passed down from generation to generation. The bishops have the authorization and anointing to keep guard over the revelation that has been deposited and to give adequate nourishment to the sheep that are under their care. This does not mean that believers should not read the Bible themselves. Quite the contrary. Ignorance of Scripture is ignorance of Christ, said Saint Jerome, the translator of the Vulgate Bible. We all need to be edified through reading the Bible. "Man shall not live by bread alone, but by every word that proceeds from the mouth of God" (Mt 4:4).

As time went by, it seemed more and more foreign to me that we should continually "rediscover the wheel" by starting the Church anew in every generation. There is a living inheritance in the Body of Christ, a precious treasure, from which to gather resources that we may rediscover and continually make use of.

I realized that the Bible and faith in its inspiration and authority do not function in isolation from the Church, into whose embrace it has been born. It should not be read in isolation from Tradition. Tradition is the oral teaching and experience of the Church through history, guided by the Holy Spirit (2 Thess 2:15). Nor can the Bible be isolated from the teaching ministry without giving rise to much arbitrariness and speculation.

We believe, pray, read, and practice the Word of God in the Church, together with all the saints of all ages. In every age, revelation must be rediscovered, appreciated, and practiced anew by us Christians. We need help to be reared in it, in order to understand it, live in it, and lovingly practice it in everyday life. This fostering is the task of the shepherds.

~

More and more questions, speculations, rumors, and complaints arose regarding our direction and new way of thinking. Anti-Catholic literature began to be printed again in Sweden.

The complaints began to pour in heavily in social media, but this did have one good effect: it forced me to deal with question after question. Those were often busy days, since I in fact had many other duties as pastor in the congregation. The interesting journey of discovery in peace and quiet in my spare time was now over. And within me a tug-of-war was being fought.

"How do you view the pope?" I was now being asked this question more and more often. Most Scandinavian Protestants do not think much about how prominently and constantly the pope figures in current affairs. But it is remarkable that one cannot find any other Christian leader, not even Billy Graham, who even comes close to the attention and influence that the pope has. When he expresses himself on some current issue, it permeates the media. His platform is unique. He speaks continually on behalf of all Christians and is readily quoted by many different Christian denominations and the news media. Whether you agree or not, you ought to listen.

To see the pope as head of the Catholic Church, the leader of the Vatican State, and the bishop of Rome was no problem for me, but this was not the issue. The question was: Is he everything that the Catholic Church claims he is?

As I mentioned earlier, I had shared the most common Protestant prejudices about the pope, and I had not thought very much about them. In recent years, my thoughts had been challenged, and my attitude changed. The question that came into focus was whether he really was the successor of Peter and not just the bishop of Rome. Does the office that the pope holds today go all the way back to the apostle Peter in a genuine line of succession? Is that necessary for the essence and function of the Church? Is the Petrine ministry a built-in structure that is there for the Church to be able to remain until Jesus returns?

If you read what Jesus himself says, and if you are prepared, despite the opposing views of many modern exegetes, to accept the Gospel of Matthew 16:18-19 as the genuine words of Jesus, then it is clear that Jesus is speaking about Peter when he speaks about the rock on which he will build his Church. Jesus says:

> And I tell you, you are Peter, and on this rock I will build my Church, and the gates of Hades shall not prevail against it. I will give you the keys of the kingdom of heaven, and whatever you bind on earth shall be bound in heaven, and whatever you loose on earth, shall be loosed in heaven.

Jesus appoints the apostle Peter to a specific ministry by giving him keys—a symbol of his authority—to bind and loose. He will do it on behalf of Jesus. It is a unique ministry, and it is to Peter alone, not to all the disciples, that Jesus speaks on this occasion.

These are radical words that Jesus directs to his disciple Peter. Throughout my entire Christian life, I had heard that these words could *not* concern the apostle Peter as a person, but pertained only to the confession that came from his mouth, "You are the Christ, the Son of the living God" (Mt 16:16). That is the standard Protestant interpretation. It would not have been possible for Luther to react against the pope if he had continued to believe, as the Church had always done, that these words of Jesus were, in fact, about the person of Peter, not only about his faith and confession.

Jesus addresses himself to Peter as a person and gives him a new name. Also, in the Gospel of John 1:42, he says: "So you are Simon the son of John? You shall be called Cephas" (which means Rock). Through the many disputes and polarized viewpoints of the Reformation, the interpretation of these words unfortunately became politicized. It became important for me to free myself of these interpretations and to try to read the text unconditionally, without mixing in reactions and conceptions that were already fixed. Once again, I realized that some interpretations depended more on what one did not *want* to believe rather than on what one, in fact, could believe.

When Jesus proclaimed the words in Matthew 16:18-19, the other disciples were standing there listening and surely associated it with the well-known passage in the Bible from the prophet Isaiah, where the Lord gave the keys of the kingdom of Judah to his master of the household. Isaiah 22:20-22 says:

> In that day I will call my servant Eliakim the son of Hilkiah, and I will clothe him with your robe, and will bind your belt on him, and will commit your authority to his hand; and he shall be a father to the inhabitants of Jerusalem and

to the house of Judah. And I will place on his shoulder the
key of the house of David; he shall open, and none shall
shut; and he shall shut, and none shall open.

The fact that Jesus refers to this passage from the Old Testament surely helped the disciples understand what it actually was all about. It was not about the king of the kingdom but, rather, about the administrator, the chamberlain,
who was elected, as one can see in the passage before these
verses. Shebna, the "master of the household" at the time,
was changed to Eliakim. The chamberlain served under the
king, but he had great authority and the keys to open and
close. Now Jesus Christ, who is the indisputable King—
the Messiah—in God's kingdom, appointed by God, gives
keys to the apostle Peter to loose and bind. Jesus himself
makes him the rock upon which he will build his Church
and delegates great authority to him, the power of the keys.

The word "rock" is used in the Bible in many different ways. In the Old Testament, the patriarch Abraham is
named as the rock out of which Israel is hewn (Is 51:1–
2). Jesus Christ is the rock, the obvious foundation (1 Cor
3:11, 10:4) upon which God's building is constructed and
from which the children of Israel prefiguratively drank when
they wandered in the desert. Jesus is the cornerstone, and
the faithful are living stones in the spiritual temple building
(1 Pet 2:4–8). Jesus says in the Sermon on the Mount that
when we build our house, our life, firmly on God's Word,
it is like building on a rock (Mt 7:24). And in Matthew
16:18, Jesus says that it is Peter, Cephas, who is the rock,
the foundation, on which the Church is built. It makes her
stable and enduring.

The context must determine what the word "rock" alludes to in the different circumstances. In the Gospel of

Matthew 16:18, it is, therefore, not a question of taking glory away from Jesus, especially since it is Jesus himself who says this to Peter. Jesus is the founder and ultimate rock of the Church, but he says himself that he delegates his authority to Peter; he lays an apostolic foundation through the ministry of Peter. In this way, Jesus builds his Church. The apostle Paul makes this distinction: "[You are] built upon the foundation of the apostles and prophets, Christ Jesus himself being the cornerstone" (Eph 2:20). One thing does not exclude the other, and what Jesus says about and to Peter is binding.

It is notable that there are clearly more references to the apostle Peter in the New Testament than to any other apostle. That is, of course, not an accident. He is spoken of far more frequently than the other twelve apostles put together. He is mentioned as Peter 154 times in the New Testament, as Simon 75 times, as Simeon two times, and as Cephas nine times. His name is first in all the lists of the apostles' names. He is present in all the important events of Jesus' life and ministry. It is only Peter among the Twelve who receives a new name given by Jesus. It is Peter who receives the revelation that Jesus is the Messiah (Mt 16:17). It is for him that Jesus prays that his faith will not fail and that he, when he has converted will strengthen his brothers (Lk 22:32).

Peter is the obvious leader after Jesus' Ascension, when the Church is born on the day of Pentecost, and likewise later when she grows and develops. In Caesarea, he also receives the unique mandate to go out and preach the Gospel to the Gentiles (Acts 10).

It was when I saw the prominent position that the apostle Peter, in fact, had in the New Testament that I realized this could not pertain solely to the beginning of the Church. There is a continuity of the Spirit in the apostolic ministry that makes the office of Peter's successor—the office of the pope—continue in the Church until the day Jesus returns. The apostolic succession is not only doctrinal succession but also succession of office.

Through this ministry of unity, the pope leads and serves the Church, and, led by the Holy Spirit, he holds her together under the Lordship of Jesus Christ. He does this together with his different collaborators, above all the bishops. Despite imperfections and sins among her members throughout a history of two thousand years, the Catholic Church remains. Jesus said that if he built his Church on Peter the rock, the gates of hell would not prevail against her, despite all attacks. The Catholic Church—despite persecutions, battles, internal and external problems, and scandals of different kinds—has nevertheless endured, faithful to Jesus' commands, for almost two thousand years now.

I realized that to humble myself and see the pope as my shepherd did not entail religious captivity, as some warned, but rather a greater freedom. It meant a greater stability and a deeper insight into the fact that one does not need to carry or do everything oneself. Instead, the Church carries us. Jesus is dwelling and present in her members.

If the Lord himself has prepared a pastoral ministry and a structure that in a flexible yet stable way preserves the Gospel and the faithful through the centuries, why did I not want to accept this? What motives were there in the depths of my soul? Of what was I actually afraid, and why could such an unwarranted irritation well up at times? Did it have to do with a struggle against the Lordship of Jesus in my own life? A hidden drive, under the mantle of "freedom", to preserve a defiant and selfish spiritual independence? Was this what caused me to prefer to criticize and keep my distance, even when I, in fact, had to admit that I did not have all the facts?

But at this point in time I started to understand that daring to submit means more than an obligatory nod to what has gone before while rushing ahead in one's own self-assured and determined way.

～

Christian unity, a true understanding of the Church, and Church history now continued to be subjects that were burning within me. I gave, among other things, a series of lectures about Church history in the evenings in our church. My wish was that our congregation would receive a greater understanding of how God has worked through his Church down through the ages. Greater knowledge of the history of the Church brings about gratitude for the Church. And the historic Church is, in fact, the Catholic Church.

～

During the year 2009, a great deal happened in our lives regarding Christian unity. In January, I was called to the General Chapter of the Bethlehem Brothers, which was held in Beit Jimal in Israel. It was certainly a new thing to me to speak to monks, and it was very stimulating for me. These were good and rewarding days with wonderful and heartfelt fellowship. They had asked me to speak about the Holy Spirit. Birgitta was also invited, and it was a true feast for us to meet with the Brothers and to be able to talk to them and tell about our different experiences. They were so open and happy. We saw here that there actually was a need even among Catholics for experience-based charismatic teaching from the Word of God about the Holy Spirit.

Back in Sweden, a few days later, we were happy to experience a renewed contact with the Swedish church, both its high-church and its charismatic branch. We were in Lund again, and I was asked to speak at the high mass at the Saint Laurentii foundation. The direction of the past years had definitely led toward coming closer to the historical churches.

In May, all the churches in Sweden got together and arranged a "Jesus Manifestation" in a central park in our capital, Stockholm. Twenty thousand Christians had gathered, and joy was in the air. Many church leaders sat on the stage, and Father Raniero Cantalamessa spoke. I am sure this was the first time most of these free-church Christians had heard a Franciscan preach, but Father Cantalamessa won their hearts. I was also invited to speak, and so did Catholic Bishop Arborelius. These Jesus Manifestations were held for a couple of years and really helped to soften some strained relations between the old and the new churches.

Later that summer I had the opportunity to come and preach at the Oasis Movement's meetings, and a friendship with its Lutheran leaders began to grow. For both Birgitta and me, it was a blessing to come closer to these groups within the Swedish church.

In August, Birgitta and I had the opportunity to visit Bishop Bertil Gärtner and his wife at their home in Onsala, south of Gothenburg, to chat. Bishop Bertil had been a professor at Princeton Theological Seminary for some years in the 1960s. Now he was confined to a wheelchair after having had a leg amputated, but he was happy and in good spirits, despite the fact that he was weak, due to illness. We had a very pleasant time, not the least because our fellowship had been completely restored again. It felt very good and precious to have this conversation with my old bishop. At the time, I did not realize that it would be the last time I would see him in this life.

On September 20, Bishop Bertil Gärtner died at the age

of eighty-four. A noble leader of our country's conservative high-church Lutherans was now gone, and he was deeply missed by many. He was so extremely loved and appreciated.

We asked ourselves who would now lead the many members in the Swedish church who did not want to go along with the liberal developments? For many years, we had often stopped our car in the Swedish countryside to go inside the old medieval churches. There, we would fall on our knees on the altar railing or in a pew and pray for the Church in Sweden: "Lord, awaken the old faith in our country! Strengthen your Church!"

At Bishop Gärtner's funeral, which filled the Gustavi cathedral in Gothenburg, I wondered to myself if Bishop Anders Arborelius would not now fill his leadership role, even for others besides Catholics. So many, both from the Swedish church and those of the free churches, look to Bishop Anders, and many have wished to consider him "their bishop". This became increasingly noticeable, especially during the so-called Jesus Manifestations in Stockholm.[1] At that time, there was a great deal of talk about how the spiritual landscape in Sweden was in the process of changing and how new types of unity that crossed over denominational borders were in the process of growing. This was something that interested me and that I thought to be very important. The Body of Christ is large, and the different members should not be isolated from one another by historical conflicts, fear, ignorance, or prejudices. I felt it was so important to overcome all forms of limitations that can so easily ensnare us.

---

[1] A gathering on a main square in Stockholm of all Christian denominations in Sweden with the unique aim of uniting Christians to bear witness together publicly to the Resurrection of Jesus.

I thought that helping out in the work for Christian unity and preparing Christians for a more difficult future was something important for me. I am convinced that increased secularization and opposition to the classical faith will force those who want to take Jesus Christ, his Gospel, and his Church seriously to come together.

~

For some time now, I had desired to take up academic studies again. After so many years out in the active ministry and after having read some theological literature on my own, it felt like it was time to begin to study again in a more structured way. So that year I contacted the professor of ecclesiology in Uppsala, Sven-Erik Brodd. Professor Brodd was very friendly and considerate toward me and—I see now in retrospect—very patient with me. I am very glad that I had this possibility

So I began to study and intended to write an essay about the New Testament understanding of "episkopē", that is, about the role of the bishop and his function. I was interested in examining how the need for spiritual leadership is expressed within Pentecostal-charismatic theology. The subject was interesting and gave me the opportunity to penetrate more deeply into the view of the sacramental ministry itself. I wanted to see how and where the two viewpoints that divide Christianity—the sacramental and the non-sacramental, respectively—harmonized and clashed.

My eagerness to study did not have the scope that it needed. As a pastor, I had many engagements and duties, which continually pressed upon me. I tried, but I did not fully succeed in giving my studies the time and concentration I had wished.

But these studies nevertheless proved to be invaluable for me in the discussions with the Vatican in which I took part at that time and where I represented the charismatic non-denominational theological viewpoint. As I mentioned earlier, I wrote the papers for our side in these informal discussions, which caused me to devour ecclesiological literature, and I learned much.

The conversations with Professor Brodd and the opportunity to participate in the research seminar at the university were a great help to me, and I am grateful for those years, from which I did profit.

~

One thing became perfectly clear to me as I neared the conclusion of my search: one cannot, in a self-willed way, accept only what fits into one's own context and way of thinking in Church history and leave aside what feels more uncomfortable.

Chapter 10

Birgitta:
Convinced, but Delaying

In the fall of 2009, we received an invitation to attend a conference in Kraków put on by a Polish Catholic charismatic organization. Ulf would be speaking alongside Father Peter Hocken. With much excitement, we accepted.

In Kraków, we stayed in the Franciscan friary where Saint Maximilian Kolbe had lived. Kolbe, who was born just before the turn of the century, was a friar on fire with zeal to spread the faith and, in particular, veneration for the Virgin Mary. He started newspapers, began to broadcast programs via radio, and also became a missionary in Japan. During the Second World War, he hid approximately two thousand Jews in a large Franciscan monastery in Niepokalanów, and when, in the end, the Nazis caught him, he was sent to Auschwitz. There, he was mistreated and whipped but was a great blessing to his fellow prisoners as a priest and fellow human being. One day, the camp guards wanted to give a lesson to the inmates and picked out ten men to starve them to death in a cellar. One of them burst into tears and wondered how his wife and small children would manage. Kolbe offered himself then to take his place, which the commander agreed to let him do. Every time the guards checked the group in the bunker, they saw Kolbe on his knees in prayer. After two weeks, he was the only one left alive, and he was then killed by a poisonous injection and cremated in one of the ovens at Auschwitz on August 15, 1941. In 1982, he was canonized by Pope John Paul II.

We stayed in a room where Kolbe had kept a printing press, and as we read about him, we felt that we were on holy ground. When one dares, as a Protestant, to step into "Catholic territory", one stumbles upon so many fantastic saints, people who lived and died for the Lord and who are shining examples for us to imitate. The friars who now lived at the friary became our dear friends. We had met some of them at the Word of Life when they participated in Ulf's leadership seminars, and, in Poland, our friendship deepened. These Franciscan Brothers and priests have opened their arms and their hearts to us in recent years, and we are so grateful for this.

The conference itself was very enriching. Many had come, both Protestants and Catholics—laity, priests, and religious. Father Hocken, an expert on the charismatic movement, was a joy to listen to. We had already read his book *The Glory and the Shame* and profited greatly from it.

It was a pleasant discovery during those days to see how open and uninhibited the Poles were in comparison with us Swedes. We often keep quiet and can feel a bit self-conscious when we are asked to speak in public gatherings. After the conference, we had a seminar out in the countryside in Lanckorona, and I was completely delighted with the young Poles' way of eagerly participating in the debate after the lectures. Those were truly enriching days.

Before we left for home, we had time to visit the monastery of Saint Faustina and the chapel where she saw Jesus many times. Faustina, as we have already told, had meant much to us early on in our journey of discovery, and it was important to come and see this place.

~

By 2010, I can safely claim that there were no questions left for me regarding the Catholic Church. Ulf had read through the entire Catechism and was lyrical over what he found. I could only wholeheartedly agree. Within me there was an "Amen" to everything I had read about in the past years: the first centuries, the origin of the Church and her continuation in history, Mary, the sacraments, the view of the Word of God, sin, eternal life, the saints—and, yes, even purgatory.

My newfound understanding of purgatory brings to mind a thought I had when the children were still at home and we were living in a house in Uppsala. We had renovated and rebuilt quite a bit, and I was delighted to have a new doorway on the side of the house leading directly into the laundry. This must have been at the end of the 1990s, before we ever gave a thought to the Catholic Church. But I said a little jokingly to Ulf: "Wouldn't it be great if heaven also had an entryway through a laundry?" I know that we are God's children, redeemed by the Blood of Jesus, but we become so dirty all the time with our daily sins. We laughed a little, but I still held on to the thought, because behind the joke there was something serious in my reflections. Heaven needs an entryway through a laundry room for all of us Christians who have not yet become perfectly sanctified, I thought.

The Bible speaks of this in 1 Corinthians 3:12–15. It says there that on that "Day" the work of each shall be tested by fire. We believe, of course, in salvation through the mighty work of Jesus' redemption on the Cross! Without him, we could never be saved from condemnation; we are washed by his Precious Blood. At the same time, we all know that we must still constantly ask for forgiveness for our sins. He cleanses us time and time again, and I believe that in the passageway between life and eternity, we may also need a cleansing in the "heavenly laundry room". This is not a punishment or a variation of hell but, rather, a grace so that we can meet our holy God face to Face, he who is himself a "consuming fire".

~

Just when spring arrived with all its loveliness, my mother's last days arrived quickly and unexpectedly. She had been born in May, and her name was Maj (May), and she was a real flower in God's Kingdom. She was determined to hang on until she turned ninety-five, and she did. But after that, her strength gave out. My siblings and I realized a little sooner than with our father that when she was bedridden at the end of May, there was no turning back. It was so painful. Once again, all my siblings and our spouses sat and grieved together. We sang for her and played peaceful, classical music. Mother was devoutly pious, simple, and natural. She was always open to other people and remembered their names. She loved classical music, especially Bach, and in her younger years, she had studied Latin. I always said to her that she could have been a linguistics professor. But she did not seek any position in this world; she wanted only to serve her beloved Jesus, so she became a missionary and a pastor's wife and a mother to five children.

When we sat around her bed that last day, one of my brothers suddenly realized that her last moment had come.

We stood up, held each other, and sang a quiet song about Jesus. When her last breath came, the dams broke in all of us. We just cried. And then we thanked God for our perfectly wonderful mother.

Even as an adult—we were all around sixty—you can feel like an orphan and really miss your parents. It is beautiful when the bond between parents and children is so strong and so full of love.

~

Despite the sorrow of my mother's passing, the summer of 2010 also contained many nice events. Ulf traveled to Wales for a conference with Church historians from many countries and came home inspired. Our son Benjamin walked on pilgrimage to Santiago de Compostela in Spain with a friend, and our son Jonathan and his wife decided to let their youngest child be baptized, having come to an appreciation of the importance of baptism. (Infant baptism is otherwise not practiced in Word of Life. Normally parents wait until the child can express his faith in Jesus.)

In July, we joined SSB (Societas Sanctae Birgittae) for the first time for its general chapter meeting in Vadstena on the feast of Saint Birgitta. SSB is a society within the Swedish Lutheran Church, and the members are what we call "high church". It was interesting and beautiful, with prayer and mass in the wonderful Blue Church that we like so much and visited so often when we acquainted ourselves with Saint Birgitta.

We also went to the Lutheran Benedictine monastery in Östanbäck, near Uppsala, when the first spade of soil was dug for the church they were planning to build, which they called the Church of Unity. Our friendship with this monastery was already being debated much in social media. The hype about us on the Internet was quite disturbing to us and especially to some members of Word of Life, and Christian newspapers kept returning to us with questions about our interest in Christian unity and in the Catholic Church. It was difficult, at times, to know how to answer.

In September, Pope Benedict XVI visited England. In Sweden, of course, his visit went unnoticed for the most part, but we followed it with interest via the BBC. England has had a unique conflict with Rome since the reign of Henry VIII. It was impressive to see how the pope was received by great crowds in Hyde Park and in many other places. The British TV commentators were so courteous in their reporting. I doubt that their Swedish colleagues would have been as nice as they were. Our friend Charles Whitehead told us later that this visit had caused a real positive change for the Catholic Church in England.

Ulf and I spoke often with each other now about the fact that we were no longer young people and that we had been in a leadership position for Word of Life for twenty-eight years. We had not yet reached the age of retirement, but we nevertheless had to begin to think seriously about the fact that the day was coming when we would have to turn the responsibility over to others.

We wanted all the congregations that Word of Life had established in different countries to have a sound theology and a responsible administration and structure. In September, we visited Word of Life in Moscow for their first Euro-Asian conference. From there, we continued to Yerevan in Armenia. With about nine thousand members, it is the largest Word of Life congregation in the whole network. They were very busy at the time building their first church, after having gathered together in sports halls for many years. It was really wonderful to see their eagerness to have a more dignified building for their congregation. We really loved our sister churches in the former Soviet Union. In city after city, we had seen a great work of evangelization grow and young leaders take responsibility to win souls for the Lord. We were so proud to be a part of this.

When I visited my work for poor children in India again in October, I went, as always, to Mother Teresa's tomb in Calcutta. It is a blessing just to sit there and think of her and pray. It is not exactly silent and peaceful in there; all kinds of sounds of the city pour in through the open windows. But that is how it should be. Mother Teresa lived in that throng of people, and despite long periods of inner torment, she always had a loving smile for the poor, the sick, and the dying. What an inspiration she has been to me!

In February 2011, I returned to India again. Ulf had been invited by the Mar Thoma Church in Kerala, a Syrian church I had heard about from my early childhood. I knew that my father and Dr. E. Stanley Jones, a great Methodist preacher and Indian missionary, had been in Kerala at Mar Thoma's great conference, which gathers nearly a hundred thousand participants every year. I remembered my father's black and white photos from the 1960s and was delighted now to be able to see this Indian church myself. We were able to meet many priests and bishops, and Ulf was honored to speak at this conference.

The Mar Thoma Syrian Church dates back to the first century, when the apostle Thomas came to evangelize on India's Malabar coast. It is fascinating to think of the long history of the Christian faith in India. Here also the Church has split into different branches, and Mar Thoma became a Protestant church in the nineteenth century. But when you see the bishops and priests, they remind you completely of

the Syrian priests that can be seen today in Jerusalem and
Södertälje, a town in Sweden with a great number of Syrian
Orthodox immigrants.

Imagine my delight when I came into the dining room
where we were to meet a bishop and on the wall over his
head we saw a beautiful painting of Brother Stanley Jones! I
told the bishop about my family's warm relationship to this
man and heard about their gratitude to this servant of God,
who preached for many years at their conference. Both my
father and Brother Stanley were very ecumenical, and now
I felt joy to walk in their footsteps.

～

Despite the joy in our work, we should have noticed that
Ulf was being forced into a tempo that was too much for
him. The pace and demands of the work were dictated, in
part, by the strain of travel. In March, Ulf flew to Porto Ale-
gre in southern Brazil for a conference. It was an exhausting
and long trip, and I realized how arduous a preaching tour
could be. After a few intense days, the conference was over,
and he flew home again and threw himself into his duties at
home. Our schedule did not often allow for the necessary
days of rest to regain our strength. This was no one's fault
but our own. We simply did not realize that the pace of our
work was too fast.

But I remember how nice it was that Easter when Ulf led
a retreat for members of our church. It became clear here
that we really had changed over the years, and there was no
doubt that Ulf's Bible meditations on Christ's Passion were
appreciated by the participants. The stillness and silence of
the retreat helped us all to penetrate more deeply into Jesus'
sacrificial death for us, and it brought healing to many. Many

were not used to silent retreats, but when they experienced it, they loved it.

The year rolled on with more work at home and more trips abroad. Despite the heartfelt love I had for the Word of Life congregation and all the fantastic people who gave all their time and energy there to serve God and help people, I could not deny that I was missing something. My heart was longing for something that I had seen in the Catholic Church. But I kept setting it aside and prayed that God would lead us wherever he willed, in his own way and his own time.

~

In August 2011, our summer vacation in Spain just happened to coincide with World Youth Day, which that year was taking place in Madrid. We felt it was an occasion we could not miss. We had heard of the pope's wonderful meetings with the world's young Catholics, and some young people from Word of Life had, in fact, been present in Cologne in 2005. So we took the train from Costa del Sol to Madrid to take part in this great event for a few days.

It was unbelievable to see the city occupied by hundreds of thousands of Christian youth! One saw them everywhere, in the metro, on the streets, and in the parks—happy, free young people who sang and played the guitar or sat munching on something good on every lawn in the city center. Pope Benedict XVI was conducting the Way of the Cross prayer service in a square, and all the large avenues around this square were totally blocked by young people who very calmly and prayerfully listened to him. On large TV screens, pictures of Jesus' Way of the Cross were being shown. I still get tears in my eyes when I think of all those young people falling on their knees everywhere on the asphalt and praying together.

The great Mass would be held at an airport outside of Madrid. We went out to the nearest metro station and then walked a few miles in a flood of people. It was hot—so hot that friendly people living in the district along our way here and there stood with hoses and sprayed water on us!

Unfortunately, we did not get into the airfield. It was packed, and several thousand of us had either to stand outside and listen or hurry home to watch the Mass on TV. More than one and a half million young people participated! We went back to the hotel and participated through television. It was an enormously beautiful and moving sight to see the devotion and reverence for Jesus among these young people.

Around that time, we spoke with some of our Catholic friends. We sought counsel from those for whom we felt great respect. What were we to do about this longing and love we felt toward the Catholic Church? How were we to handle this when we ourselves were in a leadership position in another church with a huge international network? I remember now four leading Catholics from whom we asked advice. Each of them gave the same answer: Pray, put everything in God's hands, continue forward, and see how he will lead you. None of them said that we ought to convert, that we should "follow our heart", as people often say. This alone increased our respect for the Church even more. The Church does not want a great influx of hasty, spontaneous people who will perhaps soon get new ideas and become enamored by a new spirituality.

What we really wanted at that time was to continue fostering an increased understanding in our movement toward the historical churches, primarily the Catholic Church. We saw it as ever more important and necessary for our own movement not to close its eyes but, rather, to learn about and appreciate the Church.

That fall, we led yet another group trip to Rome. As with all our trips to Rome, the opportunity to see the places of the early Church and her martyrs and to meet personally and listen to Catholics continued to break down walls in many hearts.

In November, we had a theological symposium arranged for the first time by Word of Life University. The theologians who came from abroad to be with us there were Dr. Simon Chan, Dr. Daniela Augustine, and Dr. Peter Hocken. It was a very good symposium and incredibly enriching for those who participated.

~

At the end of 2011, I had the sad experience of something serious happening to my right eye. My vision in this eye began to degenerate very quickly. A doctor told me I had a central vein thrombosis, which is to say a small blood clot in the eye's central vein. Despite surgery, the loss of vision was permanent, a rather shocking start to 2012. It was indeed a sad loss. But Ulf, our sons and their families, and many friends showed me so much love and care. To be carried by prayers is something very real and wonderful.

In the beginning, I poured coffee next to the cup, and I missed the candle that I tried to light. I still have trouble threading a needle, and I stumble on uneven surfaces that are hard to judge with one eye. And, of course, I have to resist the inner fear that my other eye will suffer the same fate. But my life is in God's hands, and I trust in him.

So, after a couple of heavy months in the beginning of 2012, it was a blessing for me to be able to travel with Ulf to Ephesus in Turkey. We had a congress there for some days with our pastors and leaders of the Word of Life congregations in the former USSR. Ongoing theological training for these pastors was something that very much engaged Ulf and his colleagues. But we also made a day's excursion to Ephesus, and it was fantastic to see this great excavated city that we had read about in the Acts of the Apostles and the letters of Saint Paul. Those dramatic scenes in the Bible now had a geographical location, and it was nothing like the flat images I had had of the city. I realized that the city is located on mountain slopes. We even drove up to the house of Mary, a little above the city. One tradition says that Saint John took her to stay with him there for a time. I am no expert on this, but it was beautiful to see the little stone house and to think of the Mother of the Lord. I could imagine how much she must have meant to the early Church, she who knew Jesus better than anyone else.

The tempo that spring had reached a fever pitch. Ulf was worn out, but his duties kept pressing on him. I myself traveled to India again to see about a new project that the Indian Children Organization was intending to sponsor. We landed in Mumbai and saw a very beautiful ministry that the Mar Thoma Church has near the brothel district. There, in those dark dwellings, are many, many small children. To imagine their lives is very painful. We had heard completely heartrending stories on an earlier visit to India. By God's grace, we could now begin to help some of these children. They are able to come to a day-care center where they can find protection, love, and care. With the consent of their mothers, they can move to a wonderful children's village out in the countryside when they are six years old.

We went out there and saw how well arranged it was, with dedicated Christian couples who took on the care of these children and began to live like a family with them in nice small houses with gardens all around. There was a Christian school, professional training for the older ones, and a church. It was very encouraging to witness this, for to protect the very poorest and those exposed to the cruelest conditions is a deep and serious calling that we all have as Christians.

For us, the last months of the school year have always been very laborious, and that spring we made trips to many countries in addition to our work at home. Ulf now had a stubborn and painful Achilles tendon infection and limped along. He nevertheless led an Easter tour to Jerusalem. On Good Friday, we walked for several hours from the Mount of Olives through Stephen's Gate and then along the whole Via Dolorosa with its fourteen stations that remind us of the painful suffering Jesus endured that day so long ago. Spiritually, it was powerful and blessed, but Ulf suffered from the pain in his heel.

In retrospect, one can see things we ought to have done differently. But at the same time, if one has promised to carry out different programs, one also has a responsibility, as a pastor, to fulfill those promises.

At the end of April, Ulf flew to the other side of the world to preach at a conference in Fiji. The church there is fantastic, a group of wonderful people who live out the mission of preaching and evangelizing. We esteem and respect them, and Ulf did not want to disappoint them by failing to come because of fatigue or a sore Achilles tendon. When he came home a few days later, he had to prepare for his annual leadership seminar. The subject that year was *Ecclesia* and *Koinonia*, new terms for many. But Ulf is a good teacher, and every year pastors came from far away to take part in the seminar. This year was no different. Ulf gave his all so that the participants would receive the spiritual nourishment they needed.

The day after the seminar, he had to hurry to another conference to give a lecture. He had dedicated much time to the study of the office of the bishop, which he has related in a previous chapter. So, he spoke about this subject, and it caught the attention of the newspaper *Dagen* (The Day) and gave the social media new fuel for the fire. Poor Word of Life was now on its way to being forced under the pope. This was the conclusion many drew.

Two days later, it was time for yet another informal meeting in Rome between nondenominational charismatic congregations and the Vatican. This time the subject was our different churches' view of both mission and suffering. Suffering was a subject that interested Ulf and me and to which we had given much thought for some years, and we had learned much through the Catholic literature we had read. The saints Padre Pio, Thérèse of Lisieux, Faustina, Bernadette, and several others had all gone through both spiritual and physical sufferings. Their holy lives and the fact that they neither rebelled against the suffering nor complained to God had disarmed us.

～

The days in Rome were strenuous for different reasons, so when we sat in the plane on the way home, we looked forward to a few nice, relaxing days in southern Sweden with our two youngest sons, who live there.

We checked into a hotel in Malmö and finally fell asleep around midnight. After we had slept for an hour, I was awakened by an awful shout from Ulf. I jumped up and called out his name in the dark. I heard him continue to shout with great effort. When I turned on the light, I saw him with wide-open eyes, his mouth half-open, a strained expression on his face. He continued to groan and neither saw nor heard me. I was very afraid and thought that he might be suffering a heart attack. So, I called his name again and again, threw myself on top of him, and made desperate attempts to help him by pressing on his chest with both hands, in a futile effort to give him heart massage. Oh, how desperately weak, small, scared, and helpless I felt. I cried out to Jesus so loudly that I might have awakened the entire hotel. But I did not care. I felt I fought with death.

Then he suddenly became quiet and completely still, his eyes wide-open and his mouth gaping. Ulf was dying before my eyes, I thought, and my grief in that moment was intense. The thought of loosing Ulf was unbearable, and I fought against it like a wild animal, resisting it with every fiber in my body. I desperately continued to press on his chest, and over and over again I cried: "Come back, come back—in Jesus' Name!" These were the worst two minutes of my life.

Suddenly he blinked and drew in a breath and looked at me, bewildered. A wave of relief fell over me, and then I began to cry, explaining to him that I thought he had died. He did not remember anything of what I described to him and was thoroughly surprised and terrified to see me so upset and sad. I tried to explain, but I realized soon that I must call an ambulance.

To my relief, the paramedics arrived quickly and loaded Ulf into the ambulance, which took us to the hospital in Malmö. Ulf seemed to recover quickly. He was weak and felt pressure in his chest, but otherwise he was fine. He smiled and talked so much that the nurse commented that he was probably in the wrong place. What was he doing in the ICU? Despite the fact that it was the middle of the night, I knew that I could call a pastor colleague in Uppsala to ask for intercessory prayers for Ulf. Wonderful doctors were now taking care of him, running a battery of tests, but neither the EKG, the brain scan, nor the EEG showed any damage from, or reasons for, what had happened. The doctors finally determined that it was "a cramp attack caused by excessive exertion". Ulf was released from the hospital by lunchtime the next day.

This traumatic experience took some time to grasp. I was sincerely grateful to God, who protected Ulf and saved him. But at nighttime he only needed to make a small sound, and I was wide awake, stiff with fear. For months I was afraid of a reoccurrence of that mysterious "cramp".

Now we had no choice. Ulf's body and soul had spoken loudly and clearly. We had to make changes and slow down the tempo of our work. It took a long time for Ulf to recover fully. At the moment I am writing this, three years have passed, and Ulf has been forced to realize that he will perhaps never have the same stamina that he had before.

The lessons we learned from the Lord through this event have been invaluable. Through the saints that I mentioned earlier and through the Catholic view of suffering, we had gained a new understanding of the ways God can teach us and form us through suffering. The normal belief in our own circles—"resist the devil and he will flee from you" (Jas 4:7)—was not sufficient anymore. By now we knew there is a lot more to say about suffering than "resist".

~

As I write about Ulf's recovery, I am reminded of the story of Naaman, the Syrian king's commander, found in 2 Kings chapter 5. Naaman needed to be healed and sought help from the prophet Elisha in Israel. But the advice he received—to wash himself in the river Jordan—was too simple for him, and he intended to ignore it. Naaman's servant, however, offered this advice: "If the prophet had commanded you to do some great thing, would you not have done it? How much rather, then, when he says to you, 'wash, and be clean'?" So Naaman obeyed and was immediately healed of his leprosy. A doctor had advised Ulf earlier to buy a certain kind of sturdy German walking boots, which would aid the healing of his Achilles tendon. Stressed as we were, we ignored the advice. How could Ulf preach in boots, anyway? But now, one week after his collapse in Malmö, we went and bought these expensive boots. Ulf wore only these shoes, and in a short time his Achilles tendon, which had tormented him for months, had healed.

Soon after that, we took the opportunity to rest for a few days at the monastery of the Sacred Heart (Heliga Hjärtas Kloster) in Omberg, a Catholic monastery for Benedictine Sisters. It was a blessing to be in silence, and the nature surrounding the monastery enticed us to go out for lovely walks along the small country roads and up the blooming slopes of Omberg Hill. The Sisters were loving, and we went home from there strengthened. We also knew by this time that we felt very much at home in the Catholic Church. But this love affair with the Church was very frustrating. "One thing you want, but another thing you must do" were words that seemed appropriate in our situation. Even though we loved and believed in the Catholic Church, we still felt a strong responsibility for our own movement.

~

After Ulf's sick leave, we traveled to our apartment in Spain, and, to our joy, we found a parish with Mass in English. The church is located in Marbella and is called Santo Cristo del Calvario, and it has become a spiritual home for us while we are in Spain. I also remember a Marian procession in Fuengirola that we just happened to see. We mingled with the crowd of people, and the feeling of solemnity and love for Mary the Mother of God was palpable. I am not a sentimental or overly emotional type, but I remember how moved I was by what I saw and experienced there. Ever since our years in Israel, Ulf and I had prayed many times for a reawakened understanding of Mary in Swedish Christianity. To venerate her is to understand the Incarnation. Mary is who she is because of Jesus. It is regrettable that such large parts of Christianity neglect Mary, for it impoverishes the faith to fail to honor her for her incomparable cooperation with God. Unfortunately, all you hear about Mary in Swedish Protestant churches is a little sermon on Christmas Eve, and that is certainly not enough.

Many times during Ulf's convalescence, we discussed what we should do about our love for the Catholic Church. What we had seen and understood was so attractive, so convincing. We have always sought the truth and have wanted to serve God with all our hearts to the best of our ability. It was sad and felt strange that we have this invisible wall in Sweden that hinders people from stepping closer to the Catholic Church and from seeing her beauty.

On our wedding anniversary in December of that year, my dear husband honored me with two gifts: the new *Catechism of the Catholic Church* and a beautiful little prayer book.

Yes, this is how we carried on. The Church drew us with a magnetic force. Jesus said to Paul, when he appeared to him on the road to Damascus, "It hurts you to kick against the goads." We were not kicking, but we resisted, since we did not know how we could be united with this beloved ancient Church when we had responsibility for another branch of the great tree of Christianity.

It must have been about that time that we saw an announcement in the *Svenska Dagbladet* (a large Swedish newspaper) about a trip to Mexico. The trip was on sale, and the time in January 2013 suited us perfectly. We had wanted to experience Mexico for many years. It is a fascinating country with an old history. The trip would include many visits to historic places where the old Aztec tribes had built their civilizations. This sounded really interesting. We also had read many years previously about the enormous number of Christian conversions that had occurred in Mexico after a remarkable vision of Mary to an Aztec man, Juan Diego, in 1531. The book we had read was *A Woman Clothed with the Sun*, by John J. Delaney. The story is too long to recount here, but what moved us and impressed us was that the event resulted in seven to nine million Indians converting and being baptized! Human sacrifice and idol worship ceased. It is an incomparable story of missionary history.

To be able to visit Mexico City and see the basilica with the image of the Virgin Mary that remains there from this event was a powerful experience. The image is an insolvable mystery and has been examined scientifically, much like the Shroud of Turin.

~

We realized now that it was not feasible for Ulf to continue as pastor. He did not have the strength, and it was not fair to the congregation, which needed an actively present pastor. So, in the beginning of the year, our board (of which we both were a part) decided that Ulf should resign in connection with Word of Life's thirty-year jubilee later in the spring. The vote for a successor fell unanimously to Joakim Lundqvist, and we decided that Ulf should take his leave in the beginning of the summer. Everyone understood Ulf's situation when this was announced to the congregation, and Pastor Joakim was received with joy. It was a great relief for us that the congregation seemed to be happy and satisfied.

In April, we again arranged a study tour to Rome for forty-five Russian-speaking pastors in our network. I remember standing in Saint Peter's Square during the Angelus prayer, listening to Pope Benedict XVI's homily, feeling so at one with what he said. How could one avoid seeing how spiritually rich and wonderful this Church was? But I had myself been so ignorant of it, and it had taken many years for me to change.

That summer we traveled around by car to the regions where Ulf and I grew up. It is true that I was born in India, but we had lived a little while in Vänersborg, my mother's hometown. We began in Skåne, the southernmost tip of Sweden, and drove north on the western side of Sweden. In one town, we stopped and went to Mass at the local Catholic Church, which Bishop Anders happened to be visiting that Sunday. After the service, we were invited home by the Fredestad family, which runs the publishing company Catholica. In recent years, many of their books had been very well received by people in our church. This contact would prove to be a lasting friendship and would even result in the publishing of this book.

It was a great day for us and for Word of Life when we had the joy of welcoming Father Raniero Cantalamessa at our "Europe conference" in July. The hearts of the people were wide open to this noble man of God. Later I heard that no conference CD sold as well that summer as did the preaching of Father Cantalamessa, who has received a special gift of reaching into the hearts of Protestants in a loving and humble way. His gift and his reception at the conference show that there are bridges on which we can walk and wavelengths on which Christians of different denominations can communicate and, in fact, comprehend and understand each other.

Directly after the conference, we traveled to Portugal for a week's vacation. On the journey, we met five wonderful Brigittine Sisters. They were from different monasteries in Sweden and Finland, and they were all originally from India, which is always an added advantage for me. We visited the village of Fatima together and saw and heard about the exceptional things that had happened there in 1916 and 1917.

Three simple shepherd children had at that time seen an angel who taught them to pray and make sacrifices for others. These prayers are so beautiful and are now prayed by millions of people around the world. One prayer is: "Oh my God, I believe, I adore, I hope, and I love Thee, and I beg pardon for all those who do not believe, do not adore, do not hope, and do not love Thee." What was interesting about these small children, all between the ages of seven to ten, was how they received in faith what they heard and held fast to it. They prayed fervently for the conversion and salvation of people. When they later saw the Virgin Mary on several occasions, she also allowed them, for a short while, to see into both heaven and hell. She also said to them that it was extremely important that people convert and pray to

God, not the least for Russia, which would otherwise spread its unbelief over great parts of the world. It is interesting that this happened to three little children in Portugal in 1917, just before the Russian Revolution . . .

But does one really need to believe in such revelations, one might wonder? The *Catechism of the Catholic Church* says in paragraph 67:

> Throughout the ages, there have been so-called "private" revelations, some of which have been recognized by the authority of the Church. They do not belong, however, to the deposit of faith. It is not their role to improve or complete Christ's definitive Revelation, but to help live more fully by it in a certain period of history. Guided by the magisterium of the Church, the *sensus fidelium* knows how to discern and welcome in these revelations whatever constitutes an authentic call of Christ or his saints to the Church.

~

Both Ulf and I now studied the Catechism together with a good priest once a month, and it was a spiritual feast every time. But it was completely unbiased. We were able to take part in the Church's instruction of the faith and then decide what this meant for us. The Psalmist says that God's Word is like pure silver, seven times refined. When I read the Catechism, I often thought that it was also like refined silver, but obviously subordinate to the Bible. For years we had seen that everything we had believed and fought for was much better formulated and described in the *Catechism of the Catholic Church* than in any other book we had read. Soon after our return home from Portugal, our youngest son, Benjamin, called us from the university town of Lund and surprised us with the news that he had now decided to become a Catholic. We were very happy for him, that he had found his true spiritual home.

Naturally, many of us in the family wanted to be with him on that day, so on November 1, we were there at Saint Thomas' church, and it was a moving and solemn moment to see our son take this important and precious step. We rejoiced that after years of study and personal searching, he had now made his decision, and it was wonderful to see him surrounded by wonderful, loving people.

In October, when I turned sixty-five, I retired. My desire to be received into the Church was now strong. There were no theological obstacles. I had for a long time now longed for the Holy Eucharist, for confession and absolution, and for the Church with apostolic Tradition and succession. Word of Life had a new pastor, and we could begin to prepare our family and our colleagues this winter for the fact that it was indeed time for us to become Catholics. It is not possible to be more convinced than we were at that time.

The prayer of Saint Birgitta: "Show me the way, and make me willing to walk in it" also has another sentence, which I now often had reason to ponder: "It is dangerous to delay, yet perilous to go forward." Yes, there are dangers of different kinds on the way to heaven, so we need to listen carefully to the Shepherd's voice in order to avoid them. But that thought—that it can also be dangerous to delay—is something we must also keep in mind.

Chapter 11

Ulf:
Time to Connect

In the spring of 2012, for the first time in my life, I sighed before the Lord and said: "Lord, help me, please take away this workload!" In recent years, I had seriously felt that the work, with all its different facets, was beginning to demand more energy than I possessed.

Our days of ecumenical talks in Rome in the month of May had been intensive but as stimulating as always. The painful inflammation in my Achilles tendon that I had suffered from for many months made every step I took painful, and we walked a lot in Rome. Afterward, a pain specialist told me that this long-lasting and intense pain could have been one of the many contributing factors to the dramatic stress attack that I now would experience.

We flew back to Sweden and spent the night in a hotel in Malmö. Our plan was to visit two of our sons who live in that part of Sweden. I did not feel particularly tired or exhausted. When Birgitta awoke to those strange sounds I made and started fighting for my life, I was having a different experience from hers. After I became conscious again, I told her what I was able to remember.

I was lying deep down in a well looking up toward the

surface of the water far above me, where I could vaguely make out a face. It was totally silent; I heard nothing, but a hand came through the water's surface, and I thought Birgitta pulled my right arm upward. I was slowly lifted up, and when I came up through the surface, I heard her calling my name. I did not understand what was happening. I was just confused and really shaken by her desperation. "Why did you pull my arm?" I asked her.

"I didn't!" she cried. "I thought you were dead!" It seemed so clear to me that Birgitta had physically pulled me up. Later I realized that she had done it in prayer, and I believe that it probably saved my life.

No physical reason at all could be found for what had happened, but my body was so tired. I was like a worn-out rag, completely finished. I was tired and exhausted, but mostly I felt sorry for Birgitta, who had undergone such an awful experience. Both Birgitta and I thank God for his help and deliverance. I am particularly grateful that this did not happen when we were abroad or when I was alone in the hotel room. I was taken to the hospital, to the intensive care unit, and was attentively taken care of. I was checked in all kinds of ways, my heart, my brain, my muscles, and so on. At first the doctor thought it was an attack of epilepsy but later ruled it out. After a few hours, a nurse came and laughingly said that they would take me out of the ICU as I looked too well and smiled too much and commented too much. Actually I felt rather good. My thinking was clear, but I felt very tired in my body. They could not find anything wrong with me, and in the late morning I was discharged from the hospital. The doctor's conclusion was that this was a case of overexertion.

Afterward, these verses from Psalm 30 came to my mind, and I was so grateful to the Lord:

I will extol you, O LORD, for you have drawn me up,
  and have not let my foes rejoice over me.
O LORD my God, I cried to you for help,
  and you have healed me. (Ps 30:1-2)

Back in Uppsala, my life had to change completely. For the most part, I lay on the sofa or took short walks. I did not feel depressed at all, but I had absolutely no energy. I had days when I seemed to have a little more energy, and I started to read a bit, but after a few lines I had to give up due to a wave of tiredness that robbed me of all ability to concentrate on the content of the book. Even very easy reading was hard. I scraped together energy to preach a sermon once at our big Europe conference in July, but otherwise it was total rest that I needed. As I slowly regained my strength, a kind of shedding was taking place within me.

For a time, I received strength and inspiration from reading the same page every day in *Five Loaves and Two Fish*, a book by the Vietnamese Bishop Francis Xavier Nguyen Van Thuan. Bishop Van Thuan had been thrown into prison by the Communists in 1975 and was there for thirteen years. For nine years he was in a solitary confinement cell. I was strongly moved by what he told:

> Above all, the long tribulation of nine years in solitary confinement, with only two guards, a mental torture, in absolute emptiness, without work, walking in the cell from morning until nine-thirty at night so as not to be destroyed by arthritis, at the edge of insanity.
>
> Many times I was tempted, tormented by the fact that I was forty-eight years old, the age of maturity; I had worked as a bishop for eight years, I had acquired much pastoral experience, and there I was: isolated, inactive, separated from my people, more than one thousand miles away!

One night I heard a voice prompting me from the depths of my heart: "Why do you torment yourself so? You have to distinguish between God and God's works. Everything you have done and want to continue doing—formation of seminarians, men and women religious, lay people, youth, building schools, the foyer for students, missions to evangelize non-Christians—all these are excellent works, God's works, but they are not God! If God wants you to abandon all these works, putting them in his hands, do it immediately, and have confidence in him. God will do it infinitely better than you; he will entrust his works to others who are much more capable than you. You have chosen God alone, not his works!"

I had always learned to do God's will. But this light brought me a new strength that completely changed my way of thinking and helped me overcome moments that were physically almost impossible.

At times a well-developed program has to be left unfinished; some activities begun with great enthusiasm are held up; large missions are demoted to minor activities. Maybe you are upset and discouraged, but has the Lord called you to follow him, or to follow this project or this person? Let the Lord work: He will work everything out for the best. . . . To choose God and not God's works: God wants me here and nowhere else.[1]

I read this again and again, and it spoke so strongly to me. Despite the fact that my external circumstances were so different from Van Thuan's, I still recognized myself in certain things. Over the course of many years, I had started up numerous different projects and activities in our movement. We had planted churches and Bible schools in many nations in the former USSR and Central Asia. I had been so focused

[1] Francis Xavier Nguyen Van Thuan, *Five Loaves and Two Fish: Meditations on the Eucharist* (London: Catholic Truth Society, 2009), 15–17.

on God's work, a large and diversified missions effort and the building of an expanding and lively congregation at the home base in Uppsala. It had been very fruitful, but here I was now, incapable of any demanding activity, and I learned that it is God—and no one and nothing else—that is important. Despite my obvious weakness, I did not have to be overcome by this. God was here; he was carrying me, and others were capable of taking care of his work.

Except for short passages from the Bible, I barely had the strength to read while I was lying there on the living room sofa. I tried to read theological literature, but it was too much for me, so I ended up reading simple marine adventure novels, the Horatio Hornblower series. I was not able to muster up more effort than that.

It took time to return to a somewhat normal life. It was not very easy for friends and acquaintances to understand how exhausted I actually was because it was not visible from the outside. The whole time I felt surrounded by God's grace but, nevertheless, very tired. It felt like inside of me a wide band stretched between two rollers had broken in the middle, and both parts had frayed. I realized that it would take time to join the band together again. My work situation would need to change in many ways.

Birgitta and I went to a Benedictine convent in Omberg. Our friend Bo Brander, a Lutheran priest, knew the Sisters and had recommended it to us. It was a wonderful experience to participate in the Liturgy of the Hours, to be surrounded by silence, and to take wonderful long walks on the mountain of Omberg, beautifully situated near one of the biggest lakes in Sweden. The view from the top was breathtaking, and all of nature during this time of midsummer was so refreshing. The Sisters were very loving, and a desire for a longer retreat began to grow in me.

So in October, I took the opportunity to return to the Bethlehem Sisters in Lourdes, where Birgitta and I had been in 2007. This time I went there alone and stayed for one week. I lived in a renovated, furnished cargo container that was like a nice cottage. The nuns were so gracious and kind to me in every way. I was mostly by myself, and I could pray, take part in the liturgy, and walk slowly by myself in the wild woods that grew on the northern slopes of the Pyrenees. It was wonderful in every way.

One day I went down to Lourdes. The evening before, alone in the little cottage, I suddenly had heard within me three sentences as I prayed: "Go to confession." "Go to Mass." "Bathe in the spring." I perceived this as a loving instruction from the Lord, and as a non-Catholic I did not know what I should do about this. It really surprised me, and it felt like an invitation to come much closer to the Catholic Church. How was I to enjoy the graces these words contained? How in the world could that happen? I was curious about what would happen in Lourdes and a bit nervous about how this would come about.

When I came down to Lourdes that day, I went around and prayed at the different places, not really knowing how I should act. I looked for the confessional area with all its booths and waited until the priests came. When I saw an Indian priest, I thought: I shall go to him. When he was free, I went up to him and introduced myself as a Protestant pastor, and he looked a little surprised but politely asked me to sit down. Then he said that since I was not Catholic, he could not give me absolution, but that we could nevertheless pray together. I was grateful for that, and then I began to bring up the sins I wanted to confess from a list I had prepared. He started eagerly to look up Bible verses and gave me well-considered, good words from the Bible for everything I mentioned. Then we prayed, and he said that it is God who forgives, and he knows the sincere regret of my heart and had heard my prayer. I took this as a form of absolution, and, incredibly happy and relieved, I left that place and spent several hours in joy and prayer in the area.

A little later, I saw that a Mass was soon about to begin in the lower church that is located near the grotto, so I went there. Crowds of Dutch people poured in, and when it was time for Communion, I stood in line together with them, not to receive Communion—I knew that I could not—but only to receive a blessing. I placed my right hand on my left shoulder as a sign that I was not Catholic. I knew that this was done in the Nordic countries, but obviously the priest did not understand this sign. Before I had time to blink, he had placed a Host in my mouth, without my being able to explain myself. I could not but receive and thank the Lord for his Body, which was food for my soul.

A little later, I stood in the long line to the bath next to the spring near the grotto. It was so beautiful to see the volunteers so thoughtfully helping all the sick who wanted to be put down into the water. All go into different booths, and there is something like a bathtub filled with ice-cold water directly from the mountain. Clothed in a thin towel, I prayed a prayer with some of the workers, and then I was dunked down into the water. Not completely dry, but very happy, I went back home to the monastery again.

The next day, I noticed that something had happened. That band I had felt was broken within me had joined together again. I felt it with absolute clarity, and it was very remarkable. From that moment, everything changed. I slowly became better and better. It was not an instant healing, but there was a definite increase in energy and my ability to concentrate. I was surrounded with a tangible sense of peace, although it still took a long time for my strength to return to normal again. I am convinced that God touched me at Lourdes. On the inside, I felt whole in a way I did not feel when I arrived. It was like broken pieces of a jar had been collected and put together, and now the jar started to fill up again. After this experience, I had more strength to resist the waves of tiredness that occasionally crashed over me. It was as if an unseen wall stopped them. There was a protection that I did not experience before my days in Lourdes. So Lourdes is definitely for me a place of true and holy miracles, and I am so unbelievably grateful for the week I was able to spend there.

~

As Birgitta has related, she had also experienced a serious attack on her health when she lost the vision in her right eye. It was very difficult for her. I admire her for being able to get through this difficulty nonetheless. She bore her suffering with such dignity and patience. She never complained, despite the fact that it entailed such distress and a great adjustment for her. The prayers of the congregation were also a great help in all of this. Birgitta has always been very respected and loved by the church members for being so genuine in her Christian life. They respected her for her passion for and involvement with the needy children of India. Despite her ailment, she kept up her courage and continued to support and encourage me.

Little by little, I became stronger, and eventually I could slowly return to my daily work. Still, everything was different. I had much time to reflect on the future. I had been away from my pastoral work for a rather long time. I realized the time had come for me to step down. I had been their pastor for almost thirty years, and for this reason alone a change would be appropriate.

After various required procedures, Joakim Lundqvist was appointed as my successor on June 2, 2013. I had been going at half-speed for exactly a year, and now I put my dear congregation in the loving hands of God and trusted that he would help and sustain the new pastor.

I still had responsibilities at Word of Life, but now I had more time to nurture my interior life and to pray seriously about the so-called "Catholic question", as it now was being called. The question had become much more urgent, and rumors, both in the media and in the church pews, were constantly going around that we were either already Catholics or would soon become so.

I thought that even I, despite the fact that I was a public person, had the right to an inner private sphere. One must have the freedom to examine one's own convictions in peace and quiet, without being forced to give answers day in and day out to every possible and impossible question and to every possible and often completely unknown questioner. I was often asked questions about issues on which I still did not have complete and full clarity. Many times I had to inform people that I was, in fact, not a Catholic and that if they wanted to debate Catholic teachings, there were Catholic theologians to whom they could turn. But to them that was not interesting; it was with me they wanted to squabble.

An image came to me: children often make pictures by drawing a line between numbered dots on a page. But it does not mean that they automatically draw the line between the right dots. If one draws these lines wrong, one can end up with a dragon instead of a beautiful horse. It felt as though some had discovered certain points, but in their haste, they had drawn the lines completely wrong and had ended up with a figment of their own imagination, instead. That they happened to see some particular point or other should not be something of which to be proud. Nor does it mean they have understood the whole story.

I really understood those who had serious questions or felt concern, and I would gladly discuss such things with them. But, on the other hand, I could not sympathize with all those who spread polemical rumors. Sometimes it became almost comical, as when the rumor spread on the Internet that the pope and I were Freemasons in collaboration with each other. It could be proven by the way I held my hand in a photo. The pope had held his in the same way on a certain occasion. The whole thing was absurd, and it was obvious that those who spread the rumors were unaware of the Catholic Church's negative stance toward Freemasonry. To navigate in these turbulent waters could be tiresome at times, especially in the aftermath of my collapse from exhaustion.

$\sim$

It is sometimes claimed that Protestant revivalist preaching is closer to the original faith and that the Catholics have, over time, distorted and added specific "Catholic dogmas", which are seen as much later insertions and additions.

In reality, it is just the opposite. It is the Catholic faith that has preserved the original faith in its historical continuity, the faith of the early Church, with the wide support of the early Church Fathers. This also includes dogmas that have been defined relatively late but that have existed since the early history of the Church. An example of this is the faith in the Real Presence in the Eucharist, the transformation of bread and wine into the Body and Blood of Jesus. The

Church has held this belief from the very beginning; it was only during the sixteenth century that it began to be denied.

It is the evangelical and charismatic revival preaching that in many aspects is responsible for modern and, from a historical perspective, later theological innovations. An example of this is the watered-down view of the Church. Another example has to do with the understanding of eschatology and the return of Jesus Christ. More and more, I saw that it was not the Catholic Church that was responsible for the collection of extra- and non-biblical dogmas. The fact was, instead, that we Protestants, in certain central aspects, were in danger of weakening, taking away, and even denying what the Church had always believed.

One area where I had to reevaluate and deepen my understanding had to do with the teaching about suffering. Of course suffering was something concrete in both our lives at this time. How to perceive suffering had been in focus for quite a long time as our perspective gradually changed. This book is not the place for a detailed discussion about that, but I can describe briefly the direction in which my thoughts were moving. The Word of Life teaching was often accused of not wanting to give any place to suffering in the Christian life. But I considered the claim that we completely denied suffering to be absurd, especially because of the fact that we were actually experiencing a great deal of suffering in the form of opposition, slander, and social harassment. Suffering was something very real for us. But this is only one type of suffering.

All people want to avoid suffering. No one wants to meet with violence, war, natural disasters, hunger, or terminal illness. A great part of our society's life is taken up both with protecting us from different forms of suffering and with relieving those who suffer.

Charismatic teaching, of which we were a part, wanted to show how the ministry of Jesus affects people's everyday lives in a supernatural and concrete way, even today. Jesus went about healing the sick. He forgave, delivered, and restored people from the most humiliating and hopeless situations. The Scriptures say that he is the same today (Heb 13:8). What we were against was a kind of teaching that, through a secular influence, in principle denied the existence of answered prayer or anything supernatural. The New Testament stories then assume a merely mythological character; they become almost like fairy tales. But the New Testament authors start out from what they believe to be historical events and encourage us to believe in divine intervention.

It is indisputable that Christians also encounter accidents, illnesses, and sometimes, in our opinion, an all too early death. The Bible does not promise total protection from suffering in this life. How are we to reconcile the idea of supernatural interventions and Jesus' promises about answers to prayer with the fact that many are nevertheless obviously still afflicted? At the same time, the New Testament clearly shows that Jesus really healed those who came to him. He warded off suffering. He also entered into suffering for our sake by his crucifixion, so that in eternity we will finally escape suffering completely. The questions that I was seeking answers to were: What had he freed us from now, and what was it that would come only in heaven?

I received help from the writings and lives of Saint Faustina, Saint Padre Pio, and Saint John Paul II in gaining a better understanding of how suffering can have meaning and can sanctify us—yes, and can even be of help to others—when we offer it to Jesus, surrender it to him, and unite it to his sufferings on the Cross. We are exhorted in the Scriptures to bear our sufferings (2 Tim 2:3) and to imitate Jesus in his sufferings (1 Pet 2:21). The Letter to the Romans 8:17 says that we are heirs with Christ if we suffer with him.

I began to understand better now the meaning of even embracing suffering and bearing it, not only of trying to be free from it. The apostle Paul says in Colossians 1:24: "Now I rejoice in my sufferings for your sake, and in my flesh I complete what is lacking in Christ's afflictions for the sake of his body, that is, the Church." This Bible verse and other similar ones had previously perplexed me—it was a completely new dimension of suffering that I had not understood.

~

In this phase I began to feel an urgent need to resolve where I was actually going, spiritually. In order to try to bring some clarity, I contacted Bishop Arborelius in February 2013 and asked to speak with him. I told him I would resign as a pastor due to my lack of energy, and I also shared my heart's desire for so much that I had seen in the Catholic Church. Our conversation led to Birgitta and me deciding to take a course of instruction in the Catholic faith, with no strings attached. We both felt that it would help us to understand the way forward. Now there was an increased longing in us to be able to join the Catholic Church at some point, not just receive more knowledge about the Catholic faith. We had read a great deal of Catholic literature but had not had the opportunity to sit down and discuss our questions about the faith with a Catholic.

The introduction courses for the Catholic faith are held in all Catholic parishes, but we could not just go down to the local parish of Saint Lars in Uppsala and sign up for one.

If we had done that, it would have been in the tabloids and
newspapers the next day, and the circus would have begun
all over again. At this point, we had already decided that we
wanted to become Catholics, but there was still a question
deep inside me about whether it would really be possible
to carry it out. I wanted to, but I was not at all sure that it
would be possible. But if it was, when?

After some time, Bishop Anders wrote to me and recommended a priest at Saint Lars parish, the Jesuit Father Ulf
Jonsson. He could see us privately and go through the *Catechism of the Catholic Church*. We would in peace and quiet be
able to ask the questions we needed and discuss the Catholic
faith. We began in the spring of 2013. Father Ulf said to us
at once that this could take up to two years. He also said that
it did not necessarily have to lead to our actually becoming
Catholic after going through the course.

With these very open conditions, we felt very good about
beginning the course. We met once a month and had several hours together, during which Father Ulf instructed us
and we asked all our questions. It was relaxed and enjoyable
and went on for about a year. It was an important time of
enlightenment, and many things fell into place.

At the same time, now that I was no longer pastor and
we were not as bound by our involvement with Word of
Life, we began to visit Swedish Catholic churches. For many
years, we had visited Catholic churches wherever we happened to be in the world. In Spain, where we often took
our vacation now, we had come in contact with an English-
speaking Catholic parish in Marbella where we felt very
much at home. We actually had more contact with Catholics outside of Sweden than we had in Sweden.

Father Ulf often had good advice to give. His ability to
lead us forward, both intellectually and spiritually, meant a

lot to us, and we are very grateful to him for all the time he gave us. When the course came to an end in February 2014, it was almost a little sad to say thank you and goodbye. It had been so enjoyable to have these theological discussions. But now we had a new phase before us. Now the idea had seriously developed and matured in us—with Birgitta, it was already a firm decision—that it was time to take the important step and come into full communion with the Catholic Church.

~

A milestone and a definitive turning point, with respect to my decision, had come during a trip to Poland in November 2013. We had been invited to a large Catholic conference in Kraków. It was not primarily charismatic, but it was ecumenical, and many charismatics were there. The theme was unity, evangelization, and the Holy Spirit. Several bishops participated, several hundred priests, religious from different Orders, and many other believers, both Catholics and Protestants. I spoke about the role of the Holy Spirit in evangelization and in the unity between Christians and about the reality of the Holy Spirit in our lives.

The conference in Kraków was marked by a wonderful atmosphere and a great hunger for God. The worship was exuberant. The evening services in a nearby basilica were particularly fantastic. To see the church packed with Christians praying and praising God so wonderfully and entering so fervently into the liturgy was very moving. There was order, freedom, devotion, courage, faith, and love in such a marvelous and mature form. At the same time, there was such a humble hunger and openness for what God does in different Christian contexts. The Anglican Bishop Sandy

Miller, who started the Alpha movement, made a fantastic contribution. A layman from Mexico, who had a large evangelizing ministry, made a great impression on me when he described concretely what Catholics call "The New Evangelization". To get to know one of Kraków's bishops, Grzegorz Ryś, who led the conference, was especially nice, and we had good and important talks.

During these very intense days with meetings from morning until evening, I felt, for the first time since my collapse, no tiredness whatsoever. During these intense days, I never felt the tiredness I had been carrying for one and a half years, a tiredness that sometimes gave me severe headaches. These symptoms would only come if I overexerted myself. I sensed they came as a warning not to jump back into excessive work again. In Poland I started to perceive that there was as a way forward for me, a community to be a part of, and even ways to serve the Lord. Now a door opened, and in the depths of my heart, I experienced that it was possible to step through it.

Some weeks after we had come home from Kraków, I contacted Pastor Joakim and told him about our thoughts and our decisions to let ourselves be received into the Catholic Church some time the following year. I also started to inform others in the leadership of Word of Life. The decision to become Catholic had now been made; but exactly when this would happen was still an open question.

It would only be natural to wonder what it was like for us to be serving at Word of Life with all these thoughts in our minds. After my collapse, I had been forced to slow down quite a bit. Birgitta had retired at this time. Even though I was no longer the pastor, I had many other positions and obligations in Word of Life, and now I made known to the leaders that I intended to retire fully in February 2014.

~

As Protestants, we easily forget how great our debt of gratitude is to the Catholic Church. To become a Catholic absolutely does not mean to be "less Christian", as some in the free-church milieu understand it to mean. No, it is about becoming a more genuine Christian. It was a deepening and anchoring in the faith that has always existed and has been preserved throughout the centuries. We were not distancing ourselves from everything we had previously stood for and done. I carry with me a great love and gratitude for what the Lord allowed us to be a part of during our years in Word of Life. I believe in God's enduring and gracious love for all his children in all Christian contexts.

When I preached for the congregation during those last years, there was so much in the treasury of the Catholic faith that I was able to use to go deeper in my preaching. I experienced it as an important time of discovery. It was also obvious at the pastors' meetings I had and at the seminar I held every year. The breadth and depth that came from these Catholic resources were appreciated by most of the attendees.

It is a great pedagogical task to instruct and inform others about the Catholic faith—which is the faith upon which we all build—not the least to Pentecostal and charismatic circles. There, much time and effort have been devoted to pointing out what separates us from the Catholics. I had been a part of this, and I believe if we would learn more about each other's faith, many prejudices would fall away and a much deeper communion would arise. Ignorance and fear are surely the greatest enemies in all of this.

We felt that our desire to become Catholics was sanctioned by the Lord, and it was deeply anchored in our hearts.

There was a clear call to take this step. But that did not mean we had a clear schedule in mind, and this question began to take up more and more of our attention. How should we inform everyone about this? We realized it would cause an upheaval, regardless of how much we prepared ourselves or tried to prepare the congregation.

Naturally, there would be howls of malicious pleasure out in the blogosphere, and some professional "know-it-alls" would burst out triumphantly: "What did we tell you?" There was nothing I could do about it; it lay outside of our control and our responsibility.

Ah well, it was not, first and foremost, to these loud critics that I was responsible; it was to the members of our congregation. After having been pastor for over thirty years, I realized that our decision to leave the movement would shake them up thoroughly. But I had complete certainty that Word of Life could handle it. It was not a question of our turning against them or rejecting everything we had built up, as some of our worst critics would wish to portray it.

It was important for me to try to show my respect for all our church members as much as possible and, in some way, as far as this could be done, to help them understand why it was necessary for us to take this step. This was not an easy task.

From the moment we announced our decision, we would find ourselves on the outside and would no longer be able to use the pulpit to preach as before in order to give further explanations and information. This would be done by others—people who perhaps did not always understand our thoughts and motives. The risk of being misunderstood was great.

There were certain groups in the congregation with backgrounds in a tradition strongly critical of Catholics. I had come across them over the years and knew that many of them were not very well grounded in theology. But we all know how easy it is, if we only scream loudly enough, to get others to believe that we know what we are talking about, and in this way fear and anger can easily spread. An unpleasant and bitter atmosphere can easily be created. In the end, we nevertheless had to trust in God in all of this. If he calls us, he will take care of us—in the same way that he takes care of all his beloved children, including those in the Word of Life movement.

At this stage, however, there was still an element of doubt in me. Perhaps we should wait one more year? Perhaps more people would then be able to understand, and perhaps the chaos would not be so great. Then something remarkable happened. I woke up one night in December, completely alert, and heard distinctly within me: "It is time to come out into the water now. How will you come, like Jonah or like Peter?" The prophet Jonah was thrown into the water, as the result of disobedience and escape. He came, in the end, to Nineveh, where the Lord called him, but only after much difficulty on the way and after three days in the belly of the whale. The apostle Peter heard Jesus' word: "Come", and he left his boat and stepped in faith out onto the water. That was also difficult. After a while, he began to sink when he saw the waves, but Jesus saved him. "I want to go the way of Peter", I thought, and fell asleep. The last bits of doubt were now finally gone.

～

We were now at the beginning of 2014, and it seemed to me that everything began to go more quickly. There was an increased tension in our church due to all the talk about us on the Internet. The few people in leadership positions who knew about our decision began to say that we could not keep delaying making it public. Ever more rumors and speculations made the situation very precarious.

We spent the month of January in our apartment in Spain, and I was writing the third part of my memoirs. At that time something very remarkable happened. Pope Francis, who for a long time had been a friend of the Anglican Bishop Tony Palmer, was requested by him to send a message to a Protestant leaders' conference in the United States. He recorded it into Tony Palmer's cell phone, and the greeting was then shown at Kenneth Copeland's leadership conference in Fort Worth, Texas. I had known Kenneth Copeland since the 1980s. I knew nothing about this event until the telephone rang in our apartment in Spain. At first, I did not want to be disturbed, but I took the telephone call anyway. Then I heard a very familiar voice. It was a young preacher whom I knew well, and he sounded very excited. The last few years we had talked a number of times on the phone about the Catholic faith, since the rumors about our interest in Catholicism were widespread. But he naturally knew nothing about our plans. He told me that he had just come out of the Copeland conference and was overwhelmed by the unexpected message from the pope. This was a group of preachers who could hardly be accused of being sympathetic to Catholics. The message hit almost like a bomb.

My friend was very strongly moved and called me as soon as the meeting was finished, and what he said really surprised me. After telling about what he had just experienced, he literally shouted into the telephone: "Ulf, you should continue on the path you have taken. You should continue doing what you are doing and proceed with the decision you have made. It is from God!" I held the telephone so that Birgitta could hear. It was quite astonishing. Our friend knew nothing about the decision we had just made.

In the end, Birgitta and I came to the conclusion, together with the board of Word of Life, that our public announcement should take place on March 9. I contacted Bishop Anders and Father Ulf, and together we eventually decided that our reception into the Catholic Church should take place on May 21.

~

Sunday, March 9 began to draw near. A press release was written and lay ready to be published on the Internet. Our TV cameras were ready to broadcast.

Many have asked me afterward if I was nervous—and the answer is both yes and no. I thought beforehand that I would be more nervous, but a great calm came over me when we sat in the car and drove the nine miles to Word of Life in silence. It was a totally unique and almost surreal situation to drive into the parking lot and go up into the room where our closest co-workers stood waiting tensely.

I had a carefully written sermon and took my time building up, step by step, to the conclusion—which came somewhere in the middle of the sermon—that Birgitta and I had decided to become Catholics.

Among other things, this is what I said:

> In essence, we can say that we have nevertheless found a continuity in the Catholic Church that goes all the way back to the apostles and Jesus himself, with a strength and stability that make the gates of hell unable to prevail against her. We believe this strength is necessary for the future and a gift to all Christians for the survival of Christianity in a

world that is becoming cruel and hostile to the Christian faith.

As a result of these discoveries, in the end, Birgitta and I realized there was a reason for the fact that we had found and appreciated all that has been preserved throughout history by the Catholic Church. It was not only in order to be a little more ecumenically educated in general; rather, we began to realize that it was, in fact, God's Spirit who was seriously prompting us to be joined to the Catholic Church. We realized more and more that he himself, in fact, guided our steps on this path.

The church was totally silent. The TV cameras captured the astonishment that ensued. Many drew in their breath. Now it had been said. After the sermon, Pastor Joakim came forward and hugged me and said some words to the congregation. When I came down from the podium, a warm applause followed that was unexpected, both by me and others. Pastor Joakim led the congregation in intercessory prayer for us and blessed us. This did not, of course, mean that everyone agreed with our decision, but it was truly a more dignified ending than I had dared to expect. But after more than thirty years of service in the Word of Life church, there was a strong bond between the members and us.

Chapter 12

Ulf: Storm Clouds and Blessings

The dignity and calm that was present at that Sunday service would not last, however. During the following days—with full attention from the media—chaos broke out within and outside the congregation. On Monday evening, we had a parish meeting where I continued to explain myself as well as answer questions. Some people were naturally quite upset. Day after day, the opinions came pouring in, and emotions were stirred up more and more. Not everyone was upset, however. There were those who accepted the news with more peace and confidence and, instead, devoted themselves to praying and trusting God.

It was not only theological concern that was expressed, but also a natural sadness and a feeling of loss. I had to remind several people again and again that I had not been the pastor of the congregation for nearly a year now, and, besides that, I had also officially retired. But naturally, this did not help, since it was a question of emotions that ran very deep. The sense of loss was something real and not easy to get over after thirty years of being together. We also felt this sense of loss. We loved our church members and did not wish to hurt them. Some began to say that we had abandoned them, even betrayed them. That was the last thing we wanted to do. Others felt accused and believed that we no longer thought they were good enough or even Christian. Some thought we had been seduced by the Catholics and had fallen away from the faith. Some came to the conclusion that we now thought that everything we had believed and stood for before was wrong. It was not that way at all, but the reaction was understandable. There were many feelings to deal with. Understandably, people wondered how we could possibly intend to take this unusual and, for many, completely unnecessary step. Could God really lead someone in our position to become Catholic? It seemed unbelievable to them.

Some could accept that the Lord had in fact called us, but in that case it would be for a kind of mission among Catholics. Someone said kindly to me that he could very well accept the fact that we would work among Catholics, but surely we could not really believe in all those "Catholic doctrines"? His astonishment was great when we said that we did, in fact, believe everything the Church teaches and that for us this was a question of truth and not just about a special path only for us.

~

We saw here what often lies beneath the surface in Sweden of today: the postmodern approach to things. This means that we say, in a relativistic way, that what is true for you is not necessarily true for me. I tolerate the choice of your path, as long as I am allowed to choose mine. Do not tell me that your truth is truer than mine. If you do, I will be hurt, perhaps offended.

According to our Christian faith, there are things that are objectively true, and the Church is in a position to safeguard and defend these objective truths—revelation—since they have a decisive significance for our salvation. The apostle Paul in 1 Timothy 3:15 says the Church is "the Church of the living God, the pillar and bulwark of the truth".

It was certainly true that the Lord had led us in a personal way on our path to the Catholic Church, but the basis for that was the fact that the Church is actually the carrier of truth, and we discovered we were in need of the Church. It was for our spiritual well-being that we needed her.

The fact that we chose to go this way did not mean that we were saying other Christians were not real Christians. But it meant, nevertheless, that we believe the Catholic Church has her roots and her authority in the mandate Jesus gave her, to be the Apostolic Church. Jesus Christ deposited the truth in all its fullness in her. Despite human defects, mistakes, temptations, and difficulties, the Church has nevertheless faithfully preserved revelation through the centuries. It was not possible for us to avoid the importance of this question of truth.

We found ourselves now in the midst of a media storm. All the main media outlets reported our decision. I had written an article in Sweden's most prominent newspaper, *Dagens Nyheter* (The Daily News). It was published on their website just when I began to preach that Sunday. I had also done an interview beforehand with the Christian newspaper *Världen i dag* (The World Today), which was published on Monday. That morning I had to get up early in order to be on two morning shows on national TV. Our conversion was discussed in many newspapers and broadcast on radio. The articles were quickly translated into English and spread on the Internet. The English newspaper *Catholic Herald* did an interview with me. So did a number of other magazines; *First Things*, *Christianity Today*, and *Charisma* all commented on our conversion. The news spread quickly everywhere. Soon friendly people from different continents wrote to us and welcomed us into the Catholic Church, which surprised us and moved us.

Now the "Catholic question" was red hot, and a media debate was beginning, not always on the highest theological level. It continued virtually every day until the day we actually were received into the Church on May 21. I have a scrapbook bulging with articles and letters to the editor covering a period of two and a half months.

During the weeks that followed, the Word of Life church was open in the evenings for members who wished to come and discuss our decision. During that time, the pastors made a great effort to try and help by answering questions and calming the concerns and confusion. We ourselves were asked to remain outside this process. This was understandable, but at the same time it created a distance that caused some who really had serious questions to believe that we were simply ignoring them and had disappeared. It was difficult for me to stand on the sidelines for the first time and not be able to help out, but it was something we had to accept. We nevertheless met many informally. Sometimes they showed up at our home, but for the most part spontaneous meetings occurred, out in town or in some shopping center. The reactions varied from hugs and tears and long conversations to being told off or to hurried steps across the street to avoid greeting us.

The week after this special Sunday, a team of co-workers from Word of Life went to Turkey in order to meet many of our pastors from the different countries in which Word of Life functions. A leadership conference was held near ancient Ephesus, and I gave a talk there, explaining to my dear brothers and sisters why we had converted. The difference now was that these people of course already knew what had happened. They had had time to digest the news. Many of them had a greater understanding of what our calling was than what I perceived in some friends back home.

I had followed many of these pastors and leaders for more than twenty years, so I was like a spiritual father to them. The meeting ended beautifully, with much love, intercessory prayer, a few tears, and many good conversations. These pastors are such fantastic people with big hearts. It was painful to leave them now, but I know they are mature leaders who stay close to God and have great spiritual experience and insight. I recalled the passage in the Acts of the Apostles when Paul left the elders in Miletus, near Ephesus, probably never to see them again.

Back home in Sweden, I sent in my last article to Word of Life's theological magazine, *Keryx*, in which I gave the reasons why we had decided to become Catholics. Now we had done what we could to explain to all our dear friends the reasons for our becoming Catholics. We had to trust God to take care of them and us.

～

At the end of March, Birgitta and I needed a break from this intense situation and went to visit our friends Charles and Sue Whitehead in England for a weekend. As we related earlier, Charles is Catholic, and Sue is an Anglican, and they have many years of experience with ecumenical work and with the tensions that can arise. They showed such love to us and to the situation of the Word of Life congregation. We had a few days of breathing space and rest. One day, we went to Littlemore outside Oxford. Littlemore was the place where John Henry Newman withdrew after he left the Anglican priesthood and became a layman. There, his decision to become a Catholic developed, and it was also there that he was received into the Catholic Church. It was very special for me to walk around and see his study, the place where he wrote some of his famous books, and to pray in his little chapel. It was rather clear that in some way we were following in his footsteps.

Back again in Uppsala, we began to prepare for a trip to Rome in April that had been scheduled a long time before with Marcus Birro, a well-known Christian author and poet. I doubted if anyone would join us on this trip, but it appeared that no one had canceled. We had a full bus, and the trip was lovely. A good thing was that we had the chance to tell about and explain our decision in peace and quiet to those who were interested. Birgitta and I were also invited to the Vatican Radio, where the Swedish journalist Charlotta Smeds interviewed us about our journey and decision. This was a nice opportunity for us to speak directly to the Swedish Catholics.

Michelle Moran and Oreste Pesare, who are president and director, respectively, of ICCRS (International Catholic Charismatic Renewal Services), invited us out to dinner one evening. We had known them for a long time, and they were both very interested in how we had come to our decision to convert. So now we had a long talk over good Italian pasta. Toward the end of the evening, Oreste asked: "Would you like to meet the pope?" What a question! Yes, but how? He could not promise anything but would scout around a little to find out. The next day we heard that after the Wednesday audience, we would be able to meet Pope Francis briefly.

We followed our group to the audience, but then we were led through another gate and ended up in the first row at the very front, just near the place where the pope sits. We sat among extremely enthusiastic Argentinians from the pope's home parish in Buenos Aires, who were also going to greet him. When the audience was over, the pope took a good amount of time and went all around in order to greet people. He began with the sick, many confined to wheelchairs, and it was striking to see how much love he showed them. Eventually he came to us.

We introduced ourselves and to our astonishment he remembered who we were and referred to his friend the Anglican Bishop Tony Palmer, who had told him about our decision. We spoke for maybe two minutes, a long time in such a line of people who were all seeking his attention. The Argentinians perhaps began to wonder how long we would actually speak with their pope. Finally, we asked for his prayers, and he immediately bowed his head, took our hands, and prayed for us silently. This felt like a really wonderful encouragement in the midst of the media storm in which we now found ourselves. We left the audience very grateful, happy, and excited about what this new life we were about to enter would mean for us.

Chapter 13

Ulf and Birgitta: Finally There!

Ulf:

What had begun as an unexpected but positive discovery many years earlier continued as something we began to appreciate and then became a definitive move toward the Catholic faith. And now we were at the point of actually being received into full communion with the Catholic Church. It felt like a tremendous grace. During the years that had passed, our attitudes had gradually changed, and the process of discovery had gone from an intellectual search to a spiritual journey that we really wanted to continue. A genuine love for Jesus in his Church had been ignited within us.

It had meant changing our position in many areas. We had not only learned to see where we had been wrong and where we had been ignorant, but we had also learned a lot regarding human nature and our own hearts. No other institution or group had shown us more about the spiritual landscape, the interior journey, the depth of the Christian faith, and the nooks and crannies of our own hearts than the Catholic Church, despite the fact that we had observed her from the outside.

If there was anything I had come to find out, it was the fact that alone one is not strong. We all have our blind spots, and now we seriously realized that we needed all the sacraments that exist in the Church. They are there at our disposal, for our help, sanctification, and salvation.

Finally, it was time to make a general confession, that is, the confession that one makes before being received into the Church and that covers one's whole life. (Confession is also called the Sacrament of Reconciliation or the Sacrament of Penance.) I knew that it was both biblical and healthy to confess one's sins before another person (Jas 5:16). We all have a tendency not to want to recognize what is really sin in our own lives, and we can easily be quick to excuse ourselves and minimize what we have done. We really need someone from the outside who can listen to us but who has also received an apostolic mission and an anointing from the Lord to mediate forgiveness for our sins in his name (Jn 20:21–23).

After having prepared ourselves as carefully as we could, we went to Saint Erik's Cathedral in Stockholm. A little nervously, we met our confessor, a priest we had never met before, Msgr. Jorge de Salas. To our relief he was very relaxed and friendly. We had each examined our consciences thoroughly and recalled the sins of which we were aware. To sift through the sins from a life of more than sixty years is not exactly an easy task, but we were counseled to concentrate on the most important things. One could easily get lost in all the details. It is better to think of the capital sins: pride, greed, envy, anger, lust, gluttony, and sloth, and what results from these sins. Most of us have secret rooms within us, the doors of which must be opened to let in the penetrating light of God's mercy. Then rivers of the blood of Jesus, pouring out of his loving heart, can cleanse us.

After having said: "I confess to Almighty God, and to you, Father, that I have sinned much in my thoughts, in

my words, in what I have done, and in what I have failed
to do", and mentioning the sins by name, it was an almost
indescribable experience to hear the words of absolution:

> God, the Father of mercies, through the death and resur-
> rection of his Son has reconciled the world to himself and
> sent the Holy Spirit among us for the forgiveness of sins;
> through the ministry of the Church may God give you par-
> don and peace, and I absolve you from your sins in the
> name of the Father, and of the Son, + and of the Holy
> Spirit. . . . The Lord has freed you from your sins. Go in
> peace.

For me, the Sacrament of Reconciliation was very special
and filled with grace. After the Eucharist, it was perhaps
in confession that I experienced the sacramental life most
clearly. As Protestant Christians, we had also confessed sins,
but it was always privately to God. It was humbling in a
deeper way to confess before another person, especially a
priest. Everything becomes very concrete, and there is no
place for excuses or blaming others. I realized what a great
grace this was on our way into the Catholic Church. A healing power through God's sacramental grace was communicated so concretely in confession that I was astonished.

Father Jorge has since then been a great help to us and
has often given us sound spiritual direction.

～

Finally May 21 arrived, the day when we would be received
into the Church and be confirmed. To avoid the attention of
the mass media, we agreed with Bishop Anders that it should
take place in peace, far from the limelight, on a day and in a
place that no one would be able to guess. He suggested the

chapel of the Brigittine Sisters in Djursholm on the outskirts of Stockholm. It was really most fitting, especially because our journey of faith toward the Church had begun with my wife Birgitta's discovery of Saint Birgitta.

It is customary to have a sponsor when one is received into the Church, and for me it was Bengt Malmgren, the doctor whom we had met in Italy in 2006. But I also had Charles Whitehead as a sponsor, since his support had been invaluable to me over the past years.

We had invited our closest family members and some friends and colleagues from Word of Life to be with us at the service. It was beautiful to have all these people around us on this occasion that was so important and revolutionary for us.

Bishop Anders was to preside at our reception ceremony into the Church, our confirmation, and the holy Mass. It was a great grace for Birgitta and me to profess the Nicene Creed, which we love, and then be able to say aloud: "I believe and profess all that the Catholic Church believes, teaches and proclaims to be revealed by God."

The bishop then anointed us with oil in the Sacrament of Confirmation, which completes and confirms the grace one has received in the Sacrament of Baptism. Confirmation is not only our confirmation of our faith, but above all it is God's confirmation of his grace in us. Through the laying on of hands and anointing with oil by the bishop, the gifts of the Holy Spirit are imparted. In the prayer he says: "Send your Holy Spirit upon them to be their helper and guide. Give them the spirit of wisdom and understanding, the spirit of right judgment and courage, the spirit of knowledge and reverence. Fill them with the spirit of wonder and awe in your presence. Through Christ our Lord." Our hearts were wide open to receive the gifts the Lord wanted to give us. Within me I heard the echo of the firm and faithful footsteps of the apostolic succession through time, all the way back to the apostles.

Now we could, for the first time as Catholics, receive the Body and Blood, Soul and Divinity of Jesus Christ in the consecrated bread and wine. The bishop, himself a Carmelite, was joined by priests from several different Orders: the Jesuits, the Oblate Fathers, the Franciscans, and the Dominicans. Some of the Brigittine Sisters were naturally also present. This important occasion was very solemn for us.

Birgitta and I also saw something symbolically important in the fact that all the priests were religious priests from different Orders. It felt as though the Catholic Church's breadth, depth, and heart were represented in a special way that evening through the six Orders that were present. The sponsors represented the active and important laity, and our invited friends represented other parts of the Body of Christ. We experienced all of this as a great, wondrous grace and also perhaps as a road sign forward. Our desire was to be in the center of the Church, in her heart, and to be involved in reaching out to all peoples with the Gospel.

Afterward, we had a wonderful time together with food and fellowship. I had the chance to thank everyone and also express our love to all, who in different ways had been a part of the steps leading up to this point in our lives. I particularly wanted to thank our friends from Word of Life who were present. Their presence was meaningful to us and served as a sign that the step we had now taken was not a distancing from them. Filled with a calm joy and a great gratitude to God, we then went home at nightfall.

Now we were finally Catholics. Naturally, totally new-born Catholics, but, nevertheless, genuine Catholics, sacramentally incorporated into the Church. The feeling of having arrived, of coming home, was clearly felt. Not in a triumphalist way, lecturing others, but as a quiet, wondrous grace and a definite strength supporting us. It is almost impossible to explain, but it was a feeling of being at home, despite all that was different and still unknown.

It was a remarkable feeling. I was now no longer a pastor but officially a layman, without any position whatsoever. Certainly we carried with us a rich experience, but at the same time there was so much that was still unfamiliar. There were things that a Catholic child knew better than we did. But it did not matter at all. The feeling of being at home nevertheless overshadowed all of this. I felt no stress about trying to grasp everything. It would be impossible even to try. I would just let it all take its time.

Birgitta:

I can only agree with everything Ulf has written above about the joy and gratitude we felt during those special days when we prepared to be received into the Catholic Church. We had finally arrived! We had come to know the Church more and more for many years now. After much prayer, Bible study, and spiritual dialogues with people in whom we had confidence, we had become convinced of the fact that we could not just stand outside. I wanted to be incorporated into her. But to believe this gives me no right to have a superior or triumphalist attitude toward other baptized and believing Christians in other denominations. I have lived in that world my whole life, and I know the spiritual treasures that exist there. But now, when I have found "one pearl of great value" (Mt 13:46), my fervent prayer is that there should be understanding and not suspicion. Jesus says that the one who seeks finds. Ulf and I had been seeking for fifteen years, and we had also spoken about it openly in articles and in Ulf's sermons and books. The seeking had led to a finding, just as the Lord said. The journey of discovery had led us to the door of the Church.

So, when we took our step through that door into the Church on May 21, 2014, it was with a prayer for the healing of the Body of Christ. Since I know how many misconceptions about the Catholic faith we ourselves had to let go of, I hope many more will dare to ask themselves the question: "Do I actually know what the Catholic Church is and teaches?"

Emotionally, there were no great fireworks shooting into the air, because it was not a question of feelings. It was about faith and about responding to the One who had carefully invited and called us for a long time. Now, when all the practical circumstances were in place and we had been able to take our decisive step, we were filled with peace and a quiet joy.

We had come full circle. What had begun for me with a book about Saint Birgitta in 2002, a book that in some ways irritated me, would lead up to the fact that we ourselves surrendered to the Lord and became Catholics. And the Lord in his goodness allowed this important event to take place with the little Sisters of Saint Birgitta in Djursholm—this was indeed wonderful!

Ulf:

What had now occurred was also a departure. When the news was released on March 9, it had already received great attention from the media. Many had their opinions about what we had done. What we felt more than the media attention, however, was the effect of our departure on the ordinary members of the Word of Life congregation Many could simply not understand.

Over the years, the congregation had grown and developed, especially through the work of many dedicated members. Here there was really involvement of the laity at its best. As I have already written, our departure was interpreted in many different ways. We wish that it had been possible to reach out to each and every one with our explanations. Our respect for all these wonderful people and for Word of Life's work is wholehearted. Despite our imperfections, I see what has developed there as something beautiful, a work of love for the Lord.

When we nevertheless now left this, it had to do with the roots and mechanisms of Protestantism. But it was not only a theoretical, theological position; we also had a sense of a deep calling.

Someone asked how I would manage when I no longer had a congregation to lead or could travel around the world doing missionary work. How would I be able to sit still in a pew? I felt, in fact, no worry whatsoever. It was, on the contrary, rather nice to be able to sit down and be one of the ordinary worshippers. What had taken hold of me, filled me, gladdened me, and nourished me deeply in this new situation was the holy Mass.

~

The Mass took hold of me like a silent storm—like a still, invisible, but clearly present power. Every time we attend Mass, I am literally drawn into the liturgy. It obviously fills a great need in me. It finds a deep echo in my inner being. Jesus is there. I experience so strongly that this is not, primarily, a service that offers a communion with other believers, even though that factor is obviously there. We are *koinonia*, a community, and we celebrate the liturgy together as God's people before him. But it is more than that. It is an incredibly deep and intimate communion with the Triune God in his holiness. We share in the Flesh and Blood of Jesus Christ.

For the reader who is not Catholic, I wish to give here a brief description of the Catholic Mass. It begins with an introductory preparation, an examination of conscience, as we humble our hearts in the confession of our sins. We call upon the Lord and ask him to have mercy on us, and we follow along in the Church's intercessory prayer, which spans the whole world. We listen to a number of texts from the Scriptures (the entire liturgy is filled with words from the Bible). Then comes the homily, and we are filled with his Word; and as a response to God's Word, the proclamation of our faith follows in the recitation of the Creed.

After the Liturgy of the Word, the Liturgy of the Eucharist follows. The Catechism explains in paragraphs 1362 and 1365: "The Eucharist is the memorial of Christ's Passover, the making present and the sacramental offering of his unique sacrifice, in the liturgy of the Church which is his Body. . . . In the Eucharist Christ gives us the very body which he gave up for us on the cross, the very blood which he 'poured out for many for the forgiveness of sins.'"[1] We then pray the Our Father, the prayer Jesus himself taught us to pray, and we give the sign of peace to each other.

And then comes Communion, where we go up and receive Jesus Christ, who comes to us in all of his sacramental presence. We eat heavenly bread, we have a share in and are united with him who has died and risen for us and whose eternal sacrifice is now re-presented—made present—for us. He satisfies our soul with himself in an unfathomable way. By eating and drinking of him, we take part in and are united with his sacrifice for us. Our offering of ourselves to him is united with his sacrifice for us.

Here I am on my knees in a simple, little church with people I hardly know, but I nevertheless have the deepest communion with them and with all Christians of all ages and with all the saints in heaven through Jesus Christ, who is now truly present in a completely special way in the Sacrament of the Eucharist. It is this sacramental presence of Jesus himself, the receiving of him and the uniting of my life with his, that has moved me so deeply.

Time and space, the present and eternity blend together. I see now why the Catholic Church has always said that the Eucharist is truly the source and summit of the Church. The worship and beholding of Jesus and participating in him and his work of salvation on Golgotha is the absolute center of the whole universe, not to mention of the Church and of my own personal life. To be led quietly and peacefully into all this is so wonderful.

These fundamental elements in the Mass—very briefly

---

[1] *Catechism of the Catholic Church*, 2nd ed. (Vatican City: Libreria Editrice Vaticana, 1997; Washington, D.C.: United States Catholic Conference, 1997), 343-44.

described here—are the foundation stones that have existed intact in the Church's liturgy since the time of the early Church. In the liturgy, we are united in a spiritual temple worship together with the whole Church through all ages and in every place, not only here on earth, but also in heaven.

To be drawn into the heavenly worship at every liturgy —however the external conditions may vary—is an amazing grace. This worship goes on continually in heaven and on earth before the throne of God—and we are invited to enter. It is so satisfying, and every time it fills me with a feeling of awe, even dread, but above all of great gratitude. Salvation becomes very real and concrete, and the Savior is very tangibly present.

I spontaneously thought of some verses in Psalm 27 which have followed me since 1970:

> One thing have I asked of the LORD,
>   that will I seek after;
> that I may dwell in the house of the LORD
>   all the days of my life,
> to behold the beauty of the LORD,
>   and to inquire in his temple. . . .
> You have said, "Seek my face."
>   My heart says to you,
> "Your face, LORD, do I seek." (Ps 27:4, 8)

Birgitta:

After our reception into the Catholic Church, our daily life changed considerably. For over thirty years we had been so deeply involved with the work of Word of Life. In this book we have tried through small glimpses to show the love and respect we have for our friends and co-workers there. Now, in one blow, we became foreigners to some of them, and that was sad. Perhaps this book can give some of them answers and explanations that we did not have the opportunity to give them. I hope so! Our hope is also that our new Catholic friends will profit from this book and see how the Lord can call and change the position of those who seem so far away.

These first weeks as Catholics were rich and eventful. The day after our reception into the Church, we went to an Oas (Oasis) meeting at a retreat center outside of Gothenburg. Both Ulf and Bishop Anders were speakers, and these services were filmed by national Swedish television and later broadcast. We celebrated our first Sunday Mass in Gothenburg, in Christ the King Catholic parish. It was special for Ulf, who had grown up in this city.

One week later we traveled to Rome. It was Pentecost, and Catholic charismatics from all over the world had a big congress in the Olympic stadium. It was fantastic to sit among fifty thousand joyful Catholics and listen to several well-known speakers. Some of them we had known before, such as our friend Charles Whitehead and his successor, Michelle Moran. But Patti Mansfield and Ralph Martin were also there from the United States, two people who have been very important for the renewal. Last but not least, Pope Francis was there, too! It was the first time a pope had participated in a charismatic meeting outside the Vatican. Everyone was exhilarated, and it was beautiful to see the pope lift his hands in praise when we all sang a song from South America that he likes: "Vive Jesus el Señor!" It was also beautiful to see him kneel at the podium and let all those thousands of people pray for him.

In his homily, he spoke about the charismatic renewal as a

great orchestra, where every instrument is different, but all are necessary for the harmony of the music. He also warned about a spirit of competition and reminded us that we all have only one leader, Jesus Christ.

After the powerful meeting in Rome, the next event was a trip to a Mass in Old Uppsala. Sunday the seventh of June was a little special for Ulf and me. Many knew about the fact that twenty-five years earlier we had been worried about Pope John Paul II's visit to Sweden. At that time, the pope had celebrated the Mass outdoors in Old Uppsala, and now Saint Lars parish was celebrating this twenty-five-year anniversary with a Mass again at the pope's stone altar near the Viking burial mounds in Old Uppsala.

Earlier in the spring, Ulf and I had already visited Old Uppsala, which is located near our home, and at that time we had stood near the altar of the pope and asked God for forgiveness for our previous negative attitude and ignorance, which had led to a distancing from the pope and the Catholic Church.

Now we came happily to this jubilee Mass, which was also our first visit to Saint Lars parish since we had become Catholics. It was so wonderful to sit there on the lawn and participate in the Mass and listen to the apostolic nuncio, Archbishop Nowacki, giving the jubilee sermon. When he passed all of us with a big smile on the way out, it felt like a little glimpse of John Paul II. They resembled each other, these two sons of Poland. Later I read that Nowacki had been ordained a priest by Karol Wojtyła, the pope-to-be, and that they had been very good friends.

That day closed yet another circle, and I was so happy and thankful that our previous unwise opposition had ended, our sin had been forgiven, and that a new period lay before us.

Saint Lars in Uppsala became our home parish, but we

also continued to visit Saint Erik's Cathedral in Stockholm now and then. It is a church we had come to like very much during our preparation period.

Ulf:

I felt that I was entering into an ever-greater reality now. I knew that it was in this environment that all future tasks could be formed. To be able to serve the Lord in the universal priesthood is what is most important. That is our deepest identity and our greatest resource; to live as children of our loving God and Father.

From this identity as children of God and in the peaceful assurance of what the essence of the Church is, the command to go out to the entire world and bear witness to Jesus Christ resounds clearly. We live for other people. To go out and preach the Gospel and to encourage the faithful to be secure in their Christian identity is still, after almost two thousand years, the command that remains until Jesus returns.

To "follow the Lamb wherever he goes," (Rev 14:4) is a spiritual adventure. It directs us both outward and inward. We are called out into the whole world in order to reach all people everywhere with the Gospel of Jesus Christ (Mt 28:18–20). This is our great mission together as Christians, as Church.

But we are also called to follow Jesus who died in order to "gather into one the children of God who are scattered abroad" (Jn 11:52). True unity is not a secondary issue for specialists. Unity is at the heart of the Gospel, in the heart of Jesus, and it affects all of us. I believe it is important for us to understand that in the harsh times that await us, we

Christians will need each other more than ever. The external opposition to our freedom, to the radical message of the Gospel, and to our way of trying to be a living witness to the love and holiness of Jesus will be challenged and questioned in an increasingly secularized world. The external pressure will then either force us together in a deeper unity or grind us down and force us to adapt to the spirit of the age. In a time such as that, it will be evident that the Catholic Church has everything necessary for the Christian faith to survive. Her openness toward other parts of the Body of Christ will then be a great blessing. It will signify the possibility of a genuine unity and a gathering around the Cross and the Savior, our Lord Jesus Christ, who has the solution to all the problems in the world.

Praised be Jesus Christ! Now and forever, Amen!

Bibliography

Colson, Charles. *The Body.* Dallas: Word Books, 1992.

Delaney, John J. *A Woman Clothed with the Sun: Eight Great Appearances of Our Lady in Modern Times.* Garden City, N.Y.: Hanover House, 1960.

Ekman, Ulf. *Andliga Rötter* (Spiritual Roots). Johanneshov: MTM, 2015.

————. *Urgamla stigar* (Ancient Paths). Uppsala: Keryx/Livets, 2014.

Glynn, Paul. *Healing Fire of Christ: Reflections on Modern Miracles—Knock, Lourdes, Fatima.* San Francisco: Ignatius Press, 2003.

Hahn, Scott. *Hail Holy Queen: The Mother of God in the Word of God.* New York: Doubleday, 2001.

————, and Kimberly Hahn. *Rome Sweet Home: Our Journey to Catholicism.* San Francisco: Ignatius Press, 1993.

Hocken, Peter. *The Glory and the Shame: Reflections on the Twentieth-Century Outpouring of the Holy Spirit.* Guildford, Surrey: Eagle, 1994.

Howard, Thomas. *Evangelical Is Not Enough: Worship of God in Liturgy and Sacrament.* San Francisco: Ignatius Press, 1988.

John Paul II. Encyclical Letter *Mother of the Redeemer* (*Redemptoris Mater*), March 25, 1987. Translation from the Vatican website.

Jørgensen, Johannes. *Saint Francis of Assisi*. London, New York: Longmans, Green, and Co., 1913.

Kreeft, Peter. *Back to Virtue: Traditional Moral Wisdom for Modern Moral Confusion*. San Francisco: Ignatius Press, 1992.

———. *Catholic Christianity*. New Haven, Conn.: Catholic Information Service, Knights of Columbus Supreme Council, 2001.

Longenecker, Dwight, and David Gustafson. *Mary: A Catholic-Evangelical Debate*. Grand Rapids, Mich.: Brazos Press, 2003.

Michalenko, Sister Sophia. *The Life of Faustina Kowalska: The Authorized Biography*. Ann Arbor, Mich.: Charis Books, 1999.

Newman, John Henry. *Apologia Pro Vita Sua: Being a History of His Religious Opinions*. Oxford: Clarendon Press, 1990.

Nguyen Van Thuan, Francis Xavier. *Five Loaves and Two Fish: Meditations on the Eucharist*. London: Catholic Truth Society, 2009.

Ratzinger, Joseph. *Introduction to Christianity*. Revised edition. San Francisco: Ignatius Press, 2004.

Ruffin, Bernard. *Padre Pio, the True Story*. Huntington, Ind.: Our Sunday Visitor, 1982.

Stinissen, Wilfrid. *Maria i Bibeln—i vårt liv*. English translation: *Mary in the Bible and in Our Lives*. San Francisco: Ignatius Press, 2018.

Weigel, George. *Witness to Hope: The Biography of Pope John Paul II*. New York: Harper Perennial, 2005.